From Field & Moor

A Country Cook's Sport

Esther
x

First published in Great Britain in 2016 by:

Broads House Publishing, Broads House Farm,
Borrowby, Thirsk, North Yorkshire, YO7 4RE.

Food photography; Dawn Caroline Smith Photography.

Cover image; 'The Captain' original art work by Tania Still.

A Cataloguing-in-Publication record for this book is available from the British Library

Designed and Printed by Orphans Press, Leominster

ISBN 978-1-5262-0355-7

Contents

Introduction

Welcome to My World

The aim is not to have a book crammed with complicated recipes, which very few of us have the patience, inclination, skill or quite frankly time to make. This book will hopefully inspire you to eat more game. It is the kind of book that you will be able to pick up and find a recipe to turn the birds shot at the weekend into an enticing supper, rather than just making pheasant casserole because you have no idea what else to do with them. Game should not be viewed as a luxury which needs complicated ingredients, only to be eaten on special occasions reserved for those part of the 'shooting set'. These days it can easily be purchased from your local butcher or branch of favourite supermarket. Game is by far and wide one of the cleanest, healthiest, and tastiest meats available.

Contrary to the assumption of most people who know me, my first memory is not of being sat on a pony, it is of cooking. Mrs Green was my grandmother, she had worked for a large shooting estate as the cook and remains something of a legend amongst those who had the privilege to spend time in her company. One of my earliest memories is being stood on a stool, so that I was tall enough to get my hands in the mixing bowl, being taught how to make 'proper pastry'. I was brought up with stories of large shooting parties lunching on the moor, and English Setters winning field trial world championships under a female dog handler. My tie with that old world still remains.

As such, cooking and field sports are in my blood. I work a small team of gun dogs on the grouse moors high up in Middleton in Teesdale and on the pheasant shoots around my farming home in North Yorkshire. This results in the inevitable freezer full of game and a true appreciation of where food comes from. Having developed an early understanding of how textures and flavours work together, combined with the irreplaceable knowledge handed down to me from Mrs Green, I have produced a collection of perfectly balanced recipes to make the most of game.

Some of the dishes are real show stoppers with a modern twist, others are just what is needed to comfort and revive you after a long, hard day, none are beyond the abilities of the average human being.

From Field & Moor will take you on a culinary journey of country sport, where you will eat fantastic food, and get an insight into a world of dogs, guns, game and rural life, through the eyes of a country girl.

Indispensable Knowledge & Understanding

*T*here are a few fundamental aspects of preparing and cooking game that, if known help not only to prevent culinary disasters, but also take food from the ordinary to the exquisite. Mrs Green taught me an awful lot, and this small section is by no means a substitute for years of experience, but that is not what we are aiming for here anyway. Arming you with the important facts and some really useful tricks will help you along the culinary adventure.

R & R

Many cookbooks and chefs emphasise the importance of allowing meat to rest once it has been cooked, before it is served. This ensures that the juices are re-distributed evenly throughout the meat and don't run out onto your plate, along with much of the flavour. It also finishes off the final bit of cooking. I agree this is very important, but equally important is relaxing the meat before you cook it. Meat is essentially muscle, if cold (i.e. from the fridge) the fibres are contracted, throw this into extreme heat to cook and you get a tough piece of meat, a culinary disaster. The meat should therefore be allowed to slowly come up to room temperature before cooking, for even something relatively small such as grouse breast they need to be removed from the fridge at least half an hour before needed. Remember, everyone needs essential R&R, relax and rest.

Identification

Know what you are working with, if you are dressing your own game: label it. My freezer is full of bags which are labelled with details such as 'Roe Foreleg, SMALL', 'Hen Pheasant Breast, badly shot', you can imagine the giggles when a friend pulled out a freezer drawer to find "Well-hung Cock, for smoking". There is no point in taking out pheasant breasts for a dish such as the Inebriated Pheasant which are damaged by shot and not intact. This meat can, nevertheless be sliced and put to good use in, for example the Thai Green Pheasant Curry.

The meat off a cock pheasant is much more robust in texture and has a deeper flavour than that off hen birds. This makes an impact on the finished dish in many recipes, not only to the taste, but also the cooking methods the meat can withstand. I would only ever smoke the breasts off cock pheasants, but feel hen pheasants are more suited to delicate dishes.

With grouse it is their age which has an enormous impact on both their value and flavour. The birds are aged by the first flight feather, which is a similar length to the next and comes to a point in a young bird of this season, in the older birds it is shortened and rounded. At the end of the day the keepers count all the shot birds to tally the bag, before sorting them into young and old.

When cooking with deer it is predominantly their species which deserves attention; "venison" is a term. There is however a huge difference in size between the saddle off a Roe and that off a Red deer, so knowing how many people you need to feed will tell you what species you require. Similarly with duck the difference between a mallard and a teal is rather imperative.

Essential information is: What it is, with details such as size, age, species, fattiness, and shot damage if appropriate, when it was killed, and how long it was hung for. If you are buying your game in a local, friendly butcher they may be able to tell you a few particulars, or game dealers such as Yorkshire Game pride themselves on details. They fully understand why I want my cocks separate from the hens!

Protection

At home we use good quality, local Dales butter from the Wensleydale Creamery for just about everything, except some baking. I fold up and save all the used paper butter wrappers as Mrs Green taught me a trick which seems to have been forgotten in modern cooking. Rather faffing on trying to spread butter onto foil, which inevitably splits, or rubbing it into the skin of game birds which then becomes damaged, use old butter wrappers to cover meat to protect it during cooking. Some butter always remains on the inside of the wrappers which adds the necessary fat, and folded out they are a perfect size and strong enough not to rip. Stored in a tub in the fridge they are ready when you are. To retain moisture I then often use an additional lid on the roasting tin, especially when cooking whole birds and joints of venison.

Jams & Jellies

Making preserves at home can be very therapeutic as well as being a great way to use gluts of fruit and vegetables. Inevitably I always have at least one batch every year which sets too hard, or soft. I will have gotten distracted and the results have gone beyond the spread on toast stage, to a solid formation not far off concrete. Despair not, this is not a culinary disaster, save the batch. As long as the contents of the jar can be extracted with a teaspoon jams and jellies which have an imperfect set are ideal for adding to sauces, as they will dissolve into the other ingredients as they are warmed. A teaspoon of damson jelly added to ordinary gravy can make it into something really special.

Equipment

Cooking utensils, especially pots and pans can cost a fortune. Some items go through fashionable phases as well. Something to remember however, is that all the fancy gadgets in the world won't make you a better cook. What is essential are heavy bottomed pans, as they distribute heat to ensure even cooking. A selection of sturdy baking trays and roasting tins, and a variety of spatulas and spoons are also a must. I cook with cast iron skillets which have been around at least 35 years, and the roasting tins belonged to my grandmother along with my treasured mixing bowls. Who knows how many batches of pastry Mrs Green made in them before me. My advice is to keep your eye out at car boot sales and in second-hand shops for old bits of kitchen equipment which were made for purpose.

For the purpose of resting meat I would recommend investing in one or two different sized wooden boards, those which have a gully around the outside to collect any free-running juices are very well designed for the job. These often come with a spike in the centre to hold meat which makes life easier during carving. The only items I have which are elaborate, but worth every single penny are my Flint and Flame knives. For anyone who is keen to dress their own game, a good quality boning knife is essential, and for me I haven't found anything better.

Salt

Use good quality salt. This may seem like an obvious statement, but it is very important as seasoning can really influence the flavour and balance of a dish. Sea salt should taste fresh and clean, the Cornish Sea Salt Company produce an excellent example of how sea salt should taste. Himalayan Pink Salt has a much more earthy flavour. It is mined in Pakistan and the colour is due to the iron oxide content of the salt, the resulting flavour is completely different. Steenbergs supply a very good selection of salts, seasonings and spices which can be ordered online. It is not that one type of salt is better than another, but each one is more suitable for different dishes. Knowing this helps to make the correct decision as to which to use when.

Alcohol

Alcohol is wonderful to cook with. The only advice to add to that is that please only ever use alcohol which is good enough to drink in your dishes, be that wine, port, brandy, whichever.

Quantities

The recipes in this book all serve different numbers of people, which can be found in each heading. If however the recipe states serves two, and you are cooking for four, simply double the quantities for all the ingredients. Pheasants and mallard serve two people per bird, all others one each. If you have over-estimated the quantities required freeze the left-overs or make something for the following night.

Proper Pastry

With some things in life it is perfectly realistic and acceptable to take a shortcut or use a little cheat, pastry is NOT one of those things. Under no circumstances can I condone the use of bought pastry. It is the first thing I remember making with Mrs Green, and nothing can beat the light, hot, flaky taste of proper pastry. There are many different types of pastry, whole books have been devoted to the subject. Essentially however, it is just flour, fat, and water. How you combine them is what makes the magic happen. I am only going to give you 2 pastry recipes; shortcrust and rough puff, as these are the most fundamental and versatile. Secrets to success are to keep the whole thing cool and airy; cold hands and atmosphere are a must, move out of a hot kitchen to make it if needs be. Ice the water, and don't rush the process, enjoy it.

Shortcrust Pastry

Ingredients

240g Plain flour

½ Teaspoon fine
sea salt

60g Vegetable fat,
such as Trex

60g Butter substitute,
such as Clover

Ice cold water

In a large, wide bowl mix the salt into the flour. Then add the 2 types of firm fats, cut them into small pieces, and coat in flour. With your fingertips rub the fats into the flour until the texture resembles tiny breadcrumbs, similar to making shortbread. Only use feathery touch between your fingertips, lifting them up and allowing the mixture to trickle down into the bowl to maintain lightness.

Now sprinkle the ice cold water, a tablespoon at a time over the pastry. Pouring straight from the jug risks the danger of too much or uneven addition of the water, either of which can ruin the pastry. After every 2 tablespoons of water, mix the pastry with a round bladed knife. Once it starts to come together and form lumps you have enough water, usually 4 or 5 tablespoons is sufficient. Gather the pastry together with your fingertips in the bowl so it forms a ball, then lift out onto a work surface dusted with a little flour and knead it just enough to form a smooth ball, again only using light pressure.

The pastry must now be wrapped in cling film or placed in a plastic bag and refrigerated at least 30 minutes before use to rest, no compromises.

Use milk to seal edges and brush the top of shortcrust pastry before cooking. Perfect for pies and tarts.

Rough Puff Pastry

Ingredients

240g Plain Flour

1 Teaspoon fine sea salt

180g Butter

150mls Ice cold water

In a large, wide bowl mix the flour and salt. Cut the butter into 1 - 1.5cm squared cubes and mix into the flour, ensuring the pieces are lightly coated before very carefully pouring in the ice cold water whilst stirring with a round bladed knife, to ensure even distribution. Gather the pastry together in the bowl and lift it out onto a surface dusted with flour. Carefully shape the pastry into a vertical rectangle and then roll out to a thickness of approximately 1 cm, with a rolling pin. As you roll you will see streaks of the yellow butter.

Fold the short sided bottom third of the pastry rectangle up, and the top third down, as if you were folding a letter, then turn the pastry to form a vertical rectangle again. Roll out and fold again. Now place the pastry in a plastic bag (something like a large, thin, sandwich bag is perfect) and refrigerate for 20 minutes to rest. After the pastry has rested repeat the rolling, folding, and turning process another twice, before resting again for 20 minutes prior to use.

Lightly beaten egg should be used to seal the edges and brush the top of rough puff pastry before cooking. Perfect for pasties and sausage rolls.

Stock

S tock is incredibly easy to make, once you know how, as such I find it an utter waste not to make a batch whenever I have cooked a whole bird or piece of venison on the bone. Admittedly, like in most farm houses I do have a vast freezer capacity. The slow simmering process used for making stock releases gelatine from the bones which gives substance to the liquid, and using stock from the correct type of game really adds depth to a dish. I would only ever combine light game birds together in a stock, for example; pheasant and partridge. Other game, such as; ducks, grouse, goose, and venison all have too strong and distinctive a flavour to be amalgamated. Be sensible with vegetables also; cabbage, broccoli, and an odd parsnip are fine to include in addition to those listed below. Potatoes will make the stock thick and cloudy, save these for the soup, and things such as turnips, fennel, and cauliflower will possibly over-power the game essence of the stock.

Ingredients

Carcass off a game
bird or remaining
venison bones

2 Celery sticks

1 White onion

3 – 4 carrots

1 – 2 Bay leaves

Bunch of a variety
of fresh herbs (e.g.
parsley, rosemary,
and thyme)

Sea salt

Black peppercorns

Remove any obvious pieces of meat from the carcass or bones, which can be used for other purposes or final addition to soup. Then place the stripped remains in a large stock / soup pan and pour over enough cold water to completely cover them. Add one teaspoon of sea salt and one of black peppercorns to the pan, and bring to the boil. Peel the onion, and slice all the vegetables before adding them to the pan along with the bay leaves and chosen herbs. Cover the pan with a loose lid, and once boiling point has been reached reduce the heat to keep the stock on a low simmer for 3 hours. Stir occasionally and top the pan up with water if the level starts to fall below the ingredients.

All the goodness and flavour will have been extracted out of the game and vegetables into the liquid. Carefully strain through a very fine sieve into clean jugs. If you are going on to make a soup straight away from the stock you may wish to pick through the residual sieve contents for any salvageable meat, there's always some. Be very careful however with bird carcasses, the bones will have become very soft during the stock making process and it is easy to end up with little fragments of bone in the meat.

If not for immediate use, allow the stock to cool and freeze in clearly labelled containers; venison stock in Pheasant and Pea Risotto won't have the desired effect! 500ml quantities are very useful to work with, they can easily be whipped out of the freezer whenever needed and de-frosted in a saucepan over a gentle heat or the microwave.

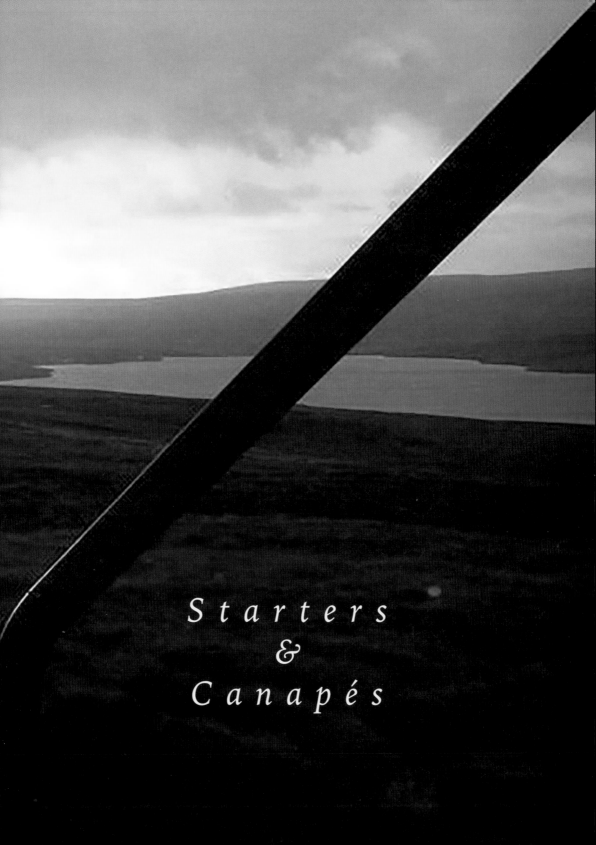

Starters
&
Canapés

Grouse Pâté

Old grouse are often an unwanted by-product of the day on the moor, people complain that the meat is tough. Like most other older things, if you treat them right, and add a little spice they turn out pretty good. The first time I tried this out on "the public" was a big birthday celebration of my mother's, graced by some keen shots and the head keeper of one of the largest Grouse Moors in England. Now I serve it ready to go on little rounds of bread as canapés, in individual ramekins as a starter, or made in a large batch for people to help themselves to at buffets or lunch. Needless to say, that first outing was a great success!

Serves Four

Ingredients

6 Grouse breasts,
preferably off old birds

Extra-virgin olive oil

150g Crème fraîche

Juice of 1 lime

Sea salt

1 teaspoon
Ginger powder

2 pinches
Cayenne pepper

For the Pâté:

Place the grouse breasts in a roasting tin, drizzle a little extra-virgin olive oil over them and cover with butter wrappers. Roast for 40 minutes, in an oven pre-heated to 180°C, removing the covering for the last 10 minutes to allow the meat to brown a little. It is fine to use any leftover meat from a whole roasted bird, but you will need to work out what it equates to in quantity for the other ingredients. Therefore I recommend not attempting this the first time you make the pâté, get a feel for consistency and flavour first.

Allow the grouse breasts to cool completely and then break into pieces. Combine with the crème fraîche, lime juice, a generous pinch of sea salt, the ginger powder and cayenne pepper, and blend until thoroughly mixed and smooth. I find my hand held stick blender, bought from a car boot sale for the princely sum of £1.- works perfectly well for this job. Taste and adjust the pâté accordingly by adding more lime juice, ginger, or cayenne pepper, but do be careful with the pepper as its flavour will strengthen over time.

Put the pâté in which ever size of ramekins you are going to use, pack it well down and smooth the top. Then cover each ramekin with cling film and refrigerate for at least 8 hours. This is important as it allows the flavours to mature and the pâté to set. You can make it the day before it is needed and the pâté will be perfect on the night.

To Serve:

Damson jelly is perfect with this, the tartness of the fruit cuts through the warm depth of the pâté. Pop it in a little bowl with a spoon and let people add their own, or just place a small amount on each canapé if preparing the ready-to-go version.

Pheasant Goujons
Served with lime mayonnaise

*Y*ou can make as many or as few of these as you want, they are incredibly quick and easy to make, and great as a snack, starter, or a big bowl full at a party. Allowing 1 breast per person gives a generous portion. The lime mayo makes it a fresh and sharp experience, which you'll want again and again.

Serves Two

Ingredients

2 Pheasant breasts

Plain flour

Sea salt

2 Eggs

2 Slices of bread
(white or wholemeal)

2 Garlic cloves

2 Tablespoons
mayonnaise

1 Tablespoon white
wine vinegar

Zest of 1 lime

For the Lime Mayonnaise:

In a bowl, beat ½ a tablespoon of white wine vinegar into the 2 tablespoons of mayonnaise. Then mix in the finely grated lime zest, reserving a sprinkling for decoration at the end, and add a generous pinch of sea salt. Taste, and add a little more of the vinegar if required. Cover the bowl with cling film and refrigerate until needed.

For the Pheasant Goujons:

Slice each pheasant breast into strips no more than 1.5cm wide. To make the breadcrumbs, break up the slices of bread, crusts and all, and place in a blender. Pulse until fine, then chop the garlic cloves very small and mix into the breadcrumbs. Take three separate bowls and put 2 tablespoons of plain flour seasoned with sea salt in the first, 2 lightly beaten eggs in the next, and in the third the garlicky breadcrumbs.

I have absolutely no health issues with deep fat fryers, we work hard enough to burn the calories off and they give the best results for dishes like this. It is much safer than using a pan, and as the fryer lives in the back-kitchen it doesn't stink the house out with the smell of cooking oil. I rest my case in defence of my Maxi-Fry! If you do not however own such an appliance, simply half fill a heavy-bottomed, high-sided frying pan with sun flower oil (or vegetable oil, but personally I prefer the flavour of sunflower oil) and heat it up to 170°C, to test the temperature; a crumb of bread dropped into the hot oil should sizzle immediately.

Take each strip of pheasant and individually roll in the flour, then dip in the egg, and finally coat in the breadcrumbs (making sure to shake off excesses after each layer), before adding to the hot oil. Be careful not to over-crowd the fryer, not only will this stop the Goujons from cooking properly, they will stick to each other. Fry for 5 minutes, then remove with the basket or a slotted spoon, and drain on kitchen paper. If you are making these in several batches, keep them warm in a bowl in the oven.

To Serve:

Transfer the lime mayonnaise into your chosen serving bowl and sprinkle the reserved lime zest on top. Place the Pheasant Goujons in a separate bowl. Then get stuck in and enjoy!

Drinking Gin and Smoking Cocks

'The Cornish', is a collective term used at home for the group of people who visit us in 'The North', for predominantly shooting purposes. They have always been known to me, and are very much part of that old world. At least one annual trip would be made to shoot grouse every year whilst they stayed on the estate my grandparents worked for, a tradition which continues today with only a variation to the lodgings. Mrs Green had a very fond relationship with 'The Cornish', and several 'small ones' were partaken in at her kitchen table along with sound advice, when maybe the beneficiaries should really have been in the company of high society.

It was about 20 years ago when I first went down to Cornwall, nothing could have prepared me for the magic of Caerhays. It was the May Bank Holiday and Mrs Green, my dear Uncle Trevor and I set off in his clapped out old Escort car. Caerhays is not only a world class shooting estate, it is a beautiful castle with a 140 acre garden boasting more than 600 species of magnolias. When we finally came up the drive the Highland cattle were grazing on the front paddocks sweeping down to the lapping sea in the cove.

Caerhays is all this, but it is also a home full of warm people who have touched and shaped my life. One such person was John Trudgeon, sadly no longer with us, with his exquisite manners and roguish smile. I'm not entirely sure what his official title on the estate was, but I saw him as the squire's right-hand man. He was also the master of getting you rather squiffy on gin, affectionately referred to as 'being Trudged'. He could make gin and tonics which slid down like nectar, but were lethal! Try this at home and you'd gag on them, as almost neat gin isn't really that palatable.

On the Sunday after our arrival we were invited for lunch at Burncoose, the main nursery for the estate, and then home to Charles and Lizzie Williams, who are now in the castle. After pleasantries and a customary gin, we sat down to eat, Lizzie promptly announced that we were having smoked cock to start! Now I was pretty wet behind the ears still then, but even I could not repress a wry smile. On further explanation it transpired that at the end of the season there were a lot of old cock pheasants hanging around that needed to be shot to allow the new intake to flourish.

After a while ideas of what to do with the meat, which can be quite strong, had started to run dry. Lizzie had come up with the ingenious idea of hot smoking the breast meat, which turned out to be delicious. Lunch progressed, as did the alcoholic beverages, including some serious sloe gin at the end of the meal.

I have never forgotten that lunch, not only because it was the first time I got drunk, and did it in style, of which Mrs Green was never made aware, but I remembered the smoked cocks, which I have re-created and made into a gorgeous starter.

Don't believe anyone who tries to tell you there is only one use for a well-hung, old cock!

Esther, Lizzie Williams and Mrs Green

Smoked Pheasant Scoops

*I*n the summer of 1981 two wonderful creations came into my father's life. An original Weber Smokey Mountain Cooker, and me. After he passed away, my mother entrusted the cooker to me. I cherish it as much as he did, as such it doesn't look its age, I hope the same can be said for me!

I would highly recommend buying some description of smoker, the Weber Smokey Mountain Cooker is still being made, it's great for smoking almost anything and doubles as a Barbeque. The depth of flavour you get from hot smoking pheasant is really enhancing, it can be adjusted by changing the variety of wood used. It's also a super way to use up well-hung birds, or old cocks! I like traditional oak smoking, and these scoops are great on big platters. The lettuce leaves serve as the vehicles for the exciting contents, and so are great to eat in your hand with a drink in the other.

Serves Eight as canapés

Ingredients

4 Pheasant breasts

Charcoal and wood
for smoking

2 Avocados

Extra-virgin Olive oil

Himalayan pink salt

Black pepper

Seeds from 1 red
pomegranate

4 Baby Gem lettuces

For the Smoked Pheasant:

Hot smoke the pheasant breasts for 2 hours, don't add any oil, salt, pepper, or anything else to the meat. I am not going to tell you here how to use the smoker, as this will depend very much on your device, so please read the manual. My advice however is; do not use firelighters or anything that may taint the meat to light the charcoal, make sure you use plenty of your chosen wood that's been soaked for at least an hour in cold water, and keep the water pan topped up.

Once your pheasant is smoked, cut the breasts with a very sharp knife across-ways into thin slices, at the most 0.5cm thick.

For the Avocado Cream:

Halve the avocados and remove their stones. Now scoop the flesh out and place in a bowl, if the fruit is ripe enough you should be able to mash it roughly with a fork. Add a generous pinch of salt, a few twist of freshly ground black pepper, and a small lug of extra-virgin olive oil (approximately 2 teaspoons). Mix and then blend into a very smooth cream. Taste it and add more seasoning and oil as necessary. People often struggle with avocado turning brown quickly, and are frightened to prepare it in advance. This happens because it reacts with light, so wrap the container holding the avocado cream entirely in tin foil and refrigerate until needed to preserve that lovely green colour.

For the Pomegranate:

Halve the pomegranate and scoop out the seeds, leaving the membrane behind. This is a bit fiddly and messy, so wear an apron as the dark red juice can stain your clothes. Or alternatively cheat; you can buy pots of pomegranate seeds from supermarkets in the fruit and veg section. They won't be as fresh as DIY and will cost more, but saves on hassle.

To assemble:

Cut the stem off the baby gem lettuces, you will probably want to discard the floppy, darker outer leaves. Separate the light green, firmer leaves to reveal little 'scoops', and rinse under cold water. Allow to dry. Take a lettuce leaf, spread about ½ a teaspoon of avocado cream in the base against the spine of the leaf, layer in 2 – 3 slices of smoked pheasant, depending on size, sticking it to the avocado, then sprinkle with pomegranate seeds to finish.

Repeat until all the ingredients are used up, serve on big platters for people to help themselves.

Partridge & Pesto Swirls

T hese are so simple to make and taste really fantastic. If you have a pizza stone cook them on it, and leave the swirls in place to serve as the stone retains heat and keeps the swirls warm for longer. They work equally well cold in a picnic hamper.

Serves Six as canapés

Ingredients

1 Pack of ready-to-bake croissant dough

100g Red pesto
(half a jar)

2 tablespoons stoned black olives

75g Cheddar cheese
(grated)

A handful of
Basil leaves

Cooked Partridge

For the Partridge:

For this quantity of swirls you will need the equivalent of 2 partridge breasts (i.e. off one bird). This is not an exact science however, so if you are using left-over meat just use roughly what you have. If the partridge needs cooking, pre-heat the oven to 180°C and cover the meat with butter wrappers, roast the breasts for 25 minutes, removing the paper for a few minutes at the end just to crisp it slightly. Allow the meat to cool and then break it up into small flakes.

For the Pesto Mixture:

I am a great advocate of simple, old fashioned utensils, pots and pans. The olives need chopping very finely for this recipe to work however, and a hand-held chopper that you stand on a board with the ingredients inside, and hit from above is just the ticket. A bit of a gadget but it does work really well, even better if you're having a bad day and need to let off some steam. In a bowl combine the pesto, grated cheese, chopped olives, shredded basil, and flaked partridge, mixing them together really well.

To Assemble the Swirls:

There should be 6 croissants in a pack, divided by perforations in the dough. Take the roll of dough out of its packaging and unroll till you have a rectangle of two croissants, then cut vertically down the perforation. Nip the diagonal perforations together and then flatten out lightly with a rolling pin so that the dough is slightly larger and thinner but retains its shape. Now spread a third of the pesto mixture on your dough and roll up horizontally. With a sharp knife cut the roll into six equal portions and place on a pizza stone or baking sheet, cut side up. Repeat with the remaining 2 rectangles of croissant dough. Make sure you leave a good gap of at least 3cm between the swirls as they are going to puff out during baking.

Bake at 180°C for 15 – 20 minutes until golden and puffed up.

Bunny Balls
Served with Roasted Sweet Pepper, Mango and Ginger Dip

N O! I am not, under any circumstances, suggesting that we fry up some rabbit's testicles as sweetbreads! They may well be the most used organ in their body, but trust me they are tiny and I'm just not in to that. These little meat balls are a combination of sweet and spicy flavours which I defy anyone not to love. If you don't have a meat grinder at home and can't find rabbit mince to buy, ask your butcher or game-dealer to mince the meat for you, which isn't a big chore however they may want more than one at a time to make it worth the effort.

Serves Four

Ingredients

Meat off one Rabbit,
haunches and loins
minced (approx. 200g)

½ teaspoon
Cumin powder

½ teaspoon
Cinnamon powder

½ teaspoon
Paprika powder

Sea Salt

Pinch of dried
Chilli flakes

1 Weetabix

1 Egg, lightly beaten

Rapeseed Oil

2 Sweet Red Peppers

1 Ripe Mango

2.5cm Piece of fresh
root Ginger

Mayonnaise

½ teaspoon
Cumin seeds

Pinch of
Cayenne Pepper

For the Bunny Balls:

Place the minced rabbit meat, cumin, cinnamon and paprika powder in a bowl with a pinch of chilli flakes and a generous few pinches of sea salt. Combine thoroughly, then crumble the Weetabix into the mixture and add the lightly beaten egg. Again mix with a wooden spoon or your hands, ensuring even distribution; you do not want any lumps of spice or Weetabix. With wet hands, this stops the meat sticking to them, take a small piece of the meat mixture and form it into a ball, compressing it together and finally rolling between your palms to get a nice round shape, aim for 3cm diameter. Place the balls on a sheet of greaseproof paper and refrigerate for at least an hour, to let the flavours develop. Remember they need to be back out of the fridge as part of their R&R before cooking.

Heat a couple of lugs of Rapeseed oil in a frying pan to fairly hot, to test that you've got it to the right temperature pop a tiny bit of meat into the oil and if it sizzles straight away; you're bang on! Carefully, as not to damage the delicate balls (sorry, no pun intended), place them in the hot oil. Fry, browning all sides for 10 minutes. Now place the bunny balls in an oven proof dish in a moderately hot oven at 180°C for another 10 minutes before serving.

For the Dip:

Wash, halve, core, and de-seed the sweet peppers, then place them on a baking sheet, cut side down, in the top of a hot oven pre-heated to 220°C, and roast for 20 minutes. The skin of the peppers should be starting to blister, and the flesh soft. Remove from the oven and place them in a glass bowl, tightly cover with cling film as this will make the peppers easier to peel once cooled. In a blender place the ripped up flesh of the cooled and peeled roasted sweet peppers, the flesh from half the mango, the peeled and chopped piece of root ginger, along with a tablespoon of mayonnaise, a little pinch of cayenne pepper, and a pinch of sea salt. Pulverise and pulse the mixture till you get a lump free consistency. Then add the cumin seeds and give it another quick whizz. Once you are happy with the seasoning, decant into a bowl and refrigerate until needed.

To Serve:

I think this works best served on individual plates, dividing the bunny balls between them, with each person getting an individual little bowl of the dip.

A far cry from sweetbreads on toast!

Gardeners' Tarts
A medley of bountiful harvest

When I think about rabbit I, like many others do have an image of Peter Rabbit sat in Mr McGregor's vegetable garden stuffing himself on radishes and such like. My grandfather was the gardener, butler, loader and any other role which was needed for the estate. He had a constant battle to endure with those pesky little visitors in order to protect his highly cherished produce. They are as much a nuisance to many country folk today as they were to him then, and that make-believe gardener tormented by their rampaging. I do think both men would definitely approve of these tarts, as they make very good use of all of the garden crop.

Serves Four

Ingredients

1 batch of short-crust pastry (see page 14)

Loins off 3 rabbits (i.e. 6 fillets)

Lemon pepper

Rapeseed oil

Broad beans

Thyme

Sour cream

Radishes

This recipe does very well as a starter but also works for canapés, they can be prepared in advance and just popped in the oven to finish off. Use a jam-tart tin and round pastry cutter to make the tarts smaller and just increase the quantities of ingredients to make as many as you want to make. To serve four as a starter I recommend individual 14cm diameter, flute edged flan tins.

For the Rabbit:

Roll each of the rabbit fillets in a little lemon pepper, Steenbergs make a fantastic version which can be sourced online. If you don't have any lemon pepper then coarse black pepper and the finely grated zest of half a lemon will work too, the lemon just adds an extra freshness to the dish. Heat a tablespoon of the rapeseed oil in a heavy bottomed frying pan over a high heat, and brown the meat for a few minutes, just enough to seal and colour it on all sides. Then lay on a board to rest.

For the Broad Bean Paste:

Add 100g of shelled broad beans (if it's out of season frozen is fine, the flavour just won't be as strong) to boiling water and simmer until tender, this will take approximately 15 minutes. Drain the beans and place in a bowl, once cooled, add a tablespoon of sour cream, the leaves off 4 sprigs of thyme, and a generous pinch of sea salt. Blend together until it turns into a smooth paste. If you find it too thick add a little more sour cream, but remember it's a paste not a cream. If you find it too bland, add a little more thyme, but be careful, as it is easy to make it too strong which will over-power the rabbit.

To Assemble the Tarts:

Roll out the prepared and suitably rested pastry to approximately 3mm thickness and line your chosen tins, which should be first dusted with plain flour to prevent the pastry sticking to them. Bake blind in an oven pre-heated to 200°C, for 15 minutes.

Spread a layer of the broad bean paste in the base of each pastry tart. Slice the rabbit fillets into approximately 1 cm pieces and divide between the four (or more) tarts, arrange the meat on top leaving one side of the tart bare. Bake in the oven for 10-15 minutes until the meat is hot and the pastry cooked, but be careful not to dry them out.

To Serve:

I did not know until recently that there are different varieties of radishes available, the lady who usually helps me in return for cooking tips, at my local fruit and vegetable stall educated me on this. The thinner, oblong shaped ones are breakfast radishes and are a good bit hotter and deeper in flavour than the usual round variety. They go very well with these tarts so do try to get hold of some. Slice 1 radish per tart very thinly and lay on the paste down the bare side of the tart, remove the tarts from the tins and you are ready to serve.

Great with a small handful of pea shoots on the side. The bright pink and green colours, with the pale meat and pastry really pop and look super, fantastic if you want to impress friends, especially if you're not sure how they will react to rabbit on the menu!

Venison & Beansprout Spring Rolls

W hen I lived down in the Cotswolds for a short period, I lodged in what had been a grand farmhouse on an old estate. Coming home in the dark up the mile long drive the deer would often run alongside your car, there were also several white stag which I often chanced upon when exercising dogs, a magical sight. Fairy tales and children's stories have not helped the general public to accept venison as part of normal food, culling wild deer is however incredibly important to keep the population healthy. As with everything, to do the animal justice we should use as much as possible. People often get a bit stuck as to what to do with the neck off a deer or the remains of a saddle which has had the loins removed. This is a perfect use! Alternatively a small piece such as shin works equally well.

Serves Four

Ingredients

150g Venison
(approximate
cooked weight)

Rapeseed oil

Sea Salt

Black pepper

300 – 500mls
Vegetable stock

2 Shallots

200g Beansprouts

Sesame oil

Light Soy sauce

1 Pack Filo
pastry sheets

There's more meat on a neck or the remains of a saddle than you would initially think. Slow cooked, the meat will just fall off the bones. If the meat yield is more than what you need for this recipe it can be frozen in batches for later use or maybe make a Game Pie or the Tomato and Venison Soup. The bones can then be boiled for stock if you want to be really prudent.

For the Venison:

Rub the venison with rapeseed oil, massaging the oil into the meat, then season with sea salt and freshly ground black pepper. Place the meat in a roasting tin, pour in enough vegetable stock to give a 1cm layer of liquid in the bottom of the tin. Peel and quarter the shallots before adding them in and then cover with a snug fitting lid or tin foil and place in the bottom of the oven, pre-heated to 125ºC. Cooking time depends on size, a small Roe neck wants 4 ½ hours and saddle off a large Red deer can easily handle 12 hours over-night. Do make sure there is enough stock in the tin to stop the meat drying out too much, and check on it every so often. About 20 minutes before the end of cooking remove the lid to allow the meat to brown slightly. Once cooked and cooled strip the meat off the bones, it should just fall away, being careful to leave any fat, ligaments, and the spinal cord behind. Don't forget to check the underside, on a saddle there is some really beautiful tender meat hiding here.

For the Spring Rolls:

Ideally in a wok, alternatively use large frying pan, heat a generous lug of sesame oil to a moderate temperature. Fry the flaked venison meat with the beansprouts, and after 1 minute add a tablespoon of light Soy sauce. Keep the mixture moving in the pan and combine the ingredients, fry for 3 more minutes, then remove from the heat.

Take one sheet of filo pastry, fold in half, and brush the edges with oil (you can use either rapeseed, sunflower, or sesame oil for this). Have the pastry vertical i.e. short sides top and bottom. Place about 10cm of venison and beansprout mixture in a horizontal line along the centre of the pastry. Fold the long sides over onto the mixture, then the bottom half into a point and up over the mixture. Then fold the top half of pastry into a point and roll the mixture tightly upwards, sealing the top point with a little oil. Be careful not to tear the fragile pastry, when complete place on a tray lined with greaseproof paper, making a total of eight spring rolls which allows two per person.

We return to the deep-fat fryer quandary. For best results deep fry these spring rolls 2 or 4 at a time, depending on the size of your fryer, at 170°C for 7 minutes so they are golden and crunchy. For a slightly 'healthier' option brush the rolls with sunflower oil and bake in the top of a hot oven at 200°C for 15 minutes.

To Serve:

Either way, serve with your favourite dipping sauce, Hoi-sin for me, whilst still piping hot.

Teal on Toast with Blueberry Sauce

I find the plumage on nearly all game birds quite fascinating, the intricate patterns and variation of colours on cock pheasants is quite something. Duck however steal the show for electric colours, as such a lot of people think of teal as a shade of green, not a game bird! The majority of meat on a teal, like a grouse, is on its breast, so admittedly at home I do just fillet them off. This is the most exquisite 'on toast'.

Serves Four

Ingredients

4 Teal breasts
(i.e. off 2 birds)

Extra-virgin Olive oil

Himalayan Pink salt

4 Slices of malted or
granary brown bread

3 – 4 Large potatoes

Double cream

Butter

100g Blueberries

1 Teaspoon
Demerara sugar

Pinch dried chilli flakes

A few scrapings very
dark chocolate

For the Potato:

Prepare a quantity of mashed potato first. Peel the potatoes and halve or quarter them as necessary, rinse, place in a pan of cold water and bring to the boil, let them bubble for 20 minutes or so until tender. Drain and steam dry before returning to the pan, add a generous knob of butter and a splash of double cream, then mash until very smooth.

Line a baking sheet with greaseproof paper and pre-heat the oven to 220°C. 20 minutes before you are ready to serve fill a piping bag which has a star nozzle with the mashed potato and pipe four 10cm diameter rounds on the baking sheet. Don't worry if there's potato left over, it's better to make too many rounds in case you break one when assembling the dish. Sprinkle with a little salt and place in the top of the oven for 10 – 15 minutes until hardening and turning brown. You can then keep them warm in the bottom of the oven until needed.

For the Blueberry Sauce:

Place the rinsed blueberries in a small pan and heat gently with a splash of water (about 20mls). As the fruit warms and slowly starts to simmer the berries will break down and form a pulp. Remove the pan from the heat and pass the fruit through a fine sieve, before returning the coulis to the pan. The acidity of fruit will react with metal utensils, so do try to use plastic, silicone or old fashioned wooden spoons etc. when dealing with fruits. Add a little knob of butter, a teaspoon of demerara sugar, tiny pinch of chilli flakes, and a scraping of the darkest chocolate you can find to the warm blueberry coulis, ensuring each dissolves into the sauce before the next addition. Keep the lovely glossy sauce warm over a low heat, taste and adjust with chilli or chocolate if necessary, and add a little boiling water if it becomes too thick.

For the Teal:

As with all meat, give the teal breasts time to relax at room temperature before you want to cook them. Massage extra-virgin olive oil into the meat and leave for 30 minutes before cooking. Rub a little salt onto all sides of each breast fillet and heat a heavy bottomed, dry, frying pan to very hot. Test the temperature by only being able to hold your hand above the base of the pan for a second when it is hot enough. Pop all four pieces of teal into the pan, press down on each for a second or two with a spatula, and turn the heat down a little. Fry for four minutes, turning every minute or so to make sure both sides of each breast fillet browns and seals without burning. Remove from the pan, lay on a board, cover with tin foil and let the meat rest for 5 minutes.

To Serve:

Toast four slices of your chosen brown bread, once done cut the crusts off to give a square of toast and butter each one lightly. Now place a potato round on top of the toast, then take each teal breast and in turn cut into 0.5cm slices across ways. Arrange on top of the potato, and finish with a trickle of blueberry sauce down the centre of the sliced meat.

Pigeon Bruschetta
with Aubergine & Tomato Salsa

L ots of people enjoy evening pigeon shooting, especially in February as it eases them out of pheasant season gently. It's quite skilled, and great fun with friends, what would you rather be doing on a Friday evening than holed up in some woods, shotgun on arm, with a motley crew, followed by a quick pint on the way home. This is much to the delight of farmers who want rid of feasting pigeons to protect their precious crops which are at a young and vulnerable stage at this time of year. Don't just throw the shot birds away though, they are actually really scrummy.

Serves Two

Ingredients

1 Aubergine

10-15 Small tomatoes

Extra-Virgin Olive oil

Sea salt

Basil leaves

Ciabatta loaf

2 Pigeon breasts
(i.e. off one bird)

Plain flour

For the Salsa:

This recipe started with this coarse salsa which was incredibly tasty, but never really had a purpose until it was introduced to pigeon. The salsa can be made up to a day in advance and refrigerated. When planning ahead do remember it takes 2 hours in the oven, but after that it's all quick and easy to concoct. Pre-heat the oven to 120ºC and wash the tomatoes and aubergine. Cut the tomatoes in half and the aubergine into 1 cm thick rounds, then arrange on a baking tray, cut side up, sprinkle with sea salt and drizzle generously with extra-virgin olive oil. Place in the oven for 2 hours to roast slowly, which will turn the tomatoes incredibly sweet and wrinkly. Remove the trays from the oven and allow to cool completely before cutting each of the aubergine rounds into 6 so that each triangle retains a piece of outer skin to hold it together. Mix the vegetables, a handful of roughly chopped basil leaves, and any oil remaining from the baking trays (or a little extra dash) in a bowl.

For the Bruschetta:

Increase the heat of the oven to full whack; up to 250ºC. Cut four 2cm thick slices from the ciabatta loaf, arrange on a baking tray, drizzle a little extra-virgin olive oil over them and place in the oven for 5 minutes until golden brown, watch they don't burn, and then set to one side.

For the Pigeon:

Take the breasts off 1 pigeon (i.e. 2 pieces of meat) and dust in plain flour. Heat a heavy bottomed frying pan until very hot, then add in a lug of extra-virgin olive oil. Place the pigeon breasts in the hot pan, turn down the heat a little, and fry for 5 minutes, turning a couple of times to ensure all sides are crispy and brown. Then rest the meat for 5 minutes on a board, before cutting each breast into six slices.

To Serve:

Arrange a spoonful of salsa on each slice of toasted ciabatta, then place 3 slices of pigeon on top. Serve two bruschetta per person as a hearty starter.

Whole Birds

Roast Grouse with Brambles

Served with Champ and Kale

T hink of the things that are in season together in that heady time of early autumn; this recipe is what I get. Shooting parties are spending long days on the moor, farmers are harvesting potatoes, and hedgerows are being scavenged for ripe fruit. Nature is very clever, as produce which ripens simultaneously often does balance very well together. Champ is a traditional Irish dish combining potatoes, spring onions known as 'scallions', milk, and butter. When I first went to Ireland, to ride horses, I couldn't understand a word people were saying to me. I watched the news three times a day, so I could follow the pictures and work the language out, soon it became second nature. I have never eaten mashed potato quite like it, and I am sure those lucky enough to have spent time there would agree. The creamy softness, goes beautifully with the sharp brambles, and whole, young grouse.

Serves Two

Ingredients

2 Young grouse, dressed

2 Shallots

Himalayan pink salt

Black pepper

100g Brambles

Ruby port

Light brown sugar

1kg Potatoes

Bunch of spring onions

100ml Milk or double cream

50g Butter

Purple or green kale

For the Grouse:

Please ensure the grouse for this dish are young, have been drawn correctly and completely, and have only been hung for a day or two. The smell of roast grouse, which has been hanging around with the crop left in for far too long is just not pleasant. I do know quite a few people who have had an aversion to these wonderful birds, simply because they were traumatised as children by over-ripe grouse. Place a peeled shallot in the cavity of each bird, then rub the outsides of the birds with a little Himalayan pink salt and twist of black pepper. Lay them in a roasting tin and pour in a splash of water along with half the brambles. Cover the birds with butter papers, and roast in the top of a pre-heated oven at 220°C for 30 minutes. Remove the butter papers and give them another 5 minutes in the top of the oven, to crisp up the skins.

For the Champ:

Wash, peel and quarter the potatoes. Place in a large pan of boiling water and cook for approximately 30 minutes, until tender. Drain the potatoes through a colander and steam dry, before returning them to the pan. Now pour in the milk or cream, add the butter, cut into pieces, and mash until completely smooth, then season with Himalayan Pink salt and freshly ground black pepper. Finally, trim and slice the spring onions and fold into the mashed potato.

For the Bramble Sauce:

Pour 100mls of port into a sauce pan and bring to the boil, allowing it to bubble away vigorously until reduced by half, then turn the heat right down to a gentle simmer. Add in the remaining brambles, with a tablespoon of light brown sugar. Carefully fold the sauce until the sugar dissolves, trying to maintain most of the brambles in shape. Continue over a gentle heat, the sauce will thicken slightly and become glossy when ready.

For the Kale:

Simply remove the tough stalks from the kale. Place the leaves in a pan of boiling water, and blanche for 4 – 5 minutes, then drain.

To Serve:

Rest the grouse for at least 10 minutes before carving, you could make the sauce during this time. Serve the carved grouse; one bird per person, on a bed of champ drizzled with bramble sauce. Kale on the side. Splendid and comforting at the same time.

Shooting party on grouse moor, including Mr Green, The Captain and Mr Julian Williams, circa 1965

Lemon Roasted Pheasant with Tarragon Sauce

Served with New Potatoes, Roasted Red Onions and Beetroot

T arragon is an incredibly fragrant herb which works very well with the acidity of the lemons and vinegars in this recipe. If you have labelled your pheasants correctly and know which are which, choose hen birds here. The result is a fresh, delicate, and perfectly balanced dish.

Serves Four

Ingredients

2 Pheasants, dressed
(preferably hen birds)

2 Lemons

Sea salt

40g Butter

40g Plain flour

500ml Milk

2 Tablespoons white
wine vinegar

Bunch of tarragon,
leaves picked and
roughly chopped

4 Beetroot

2 Red onions

2 Tablespoons
balsamic vinegar

Extra-virgin olive oil

800g New potatoes

For the Red Onions and Beetroot:

Pre-heat the oven to 180°C. Peel and rinse the beetroot, then cut each beet into about 8 wedges, depending on their size. Peel the red onions and cut into wedges a similar size to the beets. Place them together in a roasting tin, mixing them up. Sprinkle the balsamic vinegar (please don't be tempted to use the syrup version as this will not soak into the vegetables and will probably burn) evenly over the wedges. Then add a couple of lugs of extra-virgin olive oil and a sprinkling of sea salt, toss to ensure all the wedges are equally coated. Cover the tin tightly with foil and place in the bottom of the oven for 45 minutes. After this time remove the foil, toss the contents of the tin and move it up in the oven. Roast for another 30 minutes, uncovered, to slowly caramelise the vegetables.

For the Pheasants:

Wash the birds and pat dry, making sure no bits of feather remain. Cut the lemons in half and remove any visible pips, then place 2 halves inside the cavity of each bird. The juice in the lemons will release naturally during cooking to delicately flavour the meat as well as to help keep them moist. Rub the skin of the birds with a little sea salt, here I would definitely not use Himalayan pink salt as it will over-power the fragrances of tarragon and lemons, for the same reason no other herbs are added to the potatoes or vegetables. Place the birds together in a roasting tin, making sure they have been allowed to come up to room temperature first. I have two of those old-fashioned oval shaped tins with lids, a one and two bird option, which are perfect for this job. Cover each bird carefully with butter wrappers to protect the delicate skin. Then place the lid, or if you haven't got one make it out of tin foil, double covering again helps to keep the birds moist which is important here.

Place in the centre of the oven and roast at 180ºC for 30 minutes, then remove the lid, leaving the papers in place continue to roast for 15 minutes. Finally remove all the butter papers off the birds and give them a final 5 minutes or so at the top of the oven to brown. Remove the birds from the tin and place on a board, cover with foil and allow to rest for about 10 minutes before carving.

For the Sauce:

Make a basic white sauce using the roux method. If you know how to do this please crack on, if not follow these steps. You must NOT rush it, stop stirring the ingredients, or leave the pan, otherwise you will get an uncooked, lumpy, slightly burnt result.

Once mastered however it is incredibly simple:

Gently melt the 40g of butter in a saucepan. Once the butter has become liquid swirl it round the pan and then add the flour, stir the flour into the butter with a wooden spoon, beating it smooth until it has all cooked in and is starting to look like a smooth dough, this needs to take 3 minutes as a minimum to ensure it cooks. Add the milk, about 100ml at a time, stirring it into the roux, allowing it to become a smooth sauce which thickens as it comes to the boil before the next addition of milk. You may not need all the milk, or you may need a splash more, you are in charge of the temperature and liquid, get the sauce to the right consistency and then stop.

Add 2 tablespoons of white wine vinegar with a pinch of salt and beat into the sauce with your wooden spoon until thoroughly combined. Then add the chopped tarragon leaves and fold into the sauce. Just keep the sauce warm for at least 20 minutes before you are ready to eat to allow the tarragon to fully infuse and give an intense flavour. Do make sure you taste the sauce and add more tarragon or salt if required.

For the New Potatoes:

Dirty potatoes are good, they keep better and retain more flavour. If yours are dirty too, wash and scrub the skins, then add to cold water and bring to the boil. Keep at a steady boil for 20 minutes until tender, drain, steam dry, and place in a warmed bowl with a knob of salted butter.

To Serve:

Carve the pheasants onto a big serving plate, place the new potatoes, and roasted red onion and beetroot in warm bowls, and fill a jug with the tarragon sauce. Then everyone can help themselves to what they want. If you would like to include some greens, simple wilted spinach works very well, sautéed in a dry frying pan for a couple of minutes.

As children my sister and I always looked forward to getting the wishbone out of the pheasant, and a chance to ask for something special. We still do it sometimes now, although my whispered requests have changed from pony or dog, to a new rifle!

Garlicky Maple Roast Pheasant with Root Vegetables
Served with New Potatoes and Greens

*T*his is a great dish to enjoy with friends. The roasted root vegetables are like a hot cooked version of those lovely crisps you can buy. As the pheasant and roasted vegetables are quite sweet some boiled little new potatoes and simple greens like broccoli, wilted spinach or savoy cabbage go very well. A word of warning however, if the person you're sleeping with isn't eating this with you, make sure you have a spare bed for the night! Vampires will not come within a mile of you tonight!

Serves Four

Ingredients

2 Pheasants, dressed
(preferably cock birds)

2 White onions

8 Large garlic cloves

4 Sprigs of rosemary

4 Tablespoons
Maple syrup

4 Beetroot

2 Red onions

2 Tablespoons
balsamic vinegar

Thyme

4 Parsnips

4 Sweet potatoes

Himalayan Pink salt

Freshly ground
black pepper

Extra-virgin olive oil

For the Root Vegetables:

It's very important not to be tempted to cook the beetroot with the other vegetables, the whole scenario will turn pink if you do!

Peel the beetroot and red onions and cut into similar sized wedges. Place them in a roasting tin and sprinkle with the balsamic vinegar, add in 3 – 4 lugs of extra-virgin olive oil and make sure all the wedges are well coated, then rub in the Himalayan Pink salt. Place 8 – 10 sprigs of thyme in amongst the vegetables and cover the tin tightly with foil. Place in the middle of the oven, pre-heated to 180ºC for 45 minutes. Then remove the foil, turn the wedges to re-coat them in the oil and vinegar, and finish off for 30 minutes in the top of the oven.

For the sweet potatoes and parsnips, peel, dice into 2cm squared cubes or thereabouts, and coat with several lugs of extra-virgin olive oil, before rubbing the vegetables with freshly ground black pepper and the salt. Cover the roasting tin with foil and place in the oven. These need about 40 minutes with foil on, and then finished off for 20 minutes without foil. Keep an eye on the vegetables as they are roasting during that finishing off period, you just want them to be nicely golden and crispy round the edges. There's a fine line before they burn! If they are not progressing however, you could turn up the temperature of the oven once the pheasants have been removed and are resting, and finish the vegetables in the top of the oven.

For the Pheasants:

Wash the birds, making sure no bits of feather remain. Cut each onion in half and place the 2 halves inside each bird's cavity. Rub the skin with the Himalayan Pink salt, then cover each bird carefully with butter wrappers to protect the delicate meat.

Pour enough warm water into the roasting tin to give 0.5cm depth, then add the whole, peeled garlic cloves and finely chopped rosemary. Now lay the pheasants, side by side in the tin, I have one and two bird sized old fashioned, oval shaped ones with lids which are excellent for roasting whole birds. Cover the tin with a tight fitting lid and roast at 180°C for 45 minutes. Remove the lid and papers off the birds after 45 minutes and baste with the cooking liquid, being careful not to break up the garlic. Return to the oven for 5 minutes or so, until golden. Remove the birds from the tin and place on a board to rest.

For the Maple Sauce:

Heat the juices, rosemary and garlic cloves, which remain in the roasting tin on the hob to boiling point and bubble until reduced by half. Squish up the garlic cloves which will incorporate into the sauce. Then add 2 tablespoons of maple syrup and beat into the jus with a hand whisk or wooden spoon, continuing to let it bubble until you reach a nice consistency for pouring sauce, then transfer into a warmed jug.

To Serve:

Place the roasted root vegetables together and serve alongside carved slices of pheasant, with buttered hot new potatoes and greens to your liking.

Game Girls
Served with a Little Bravado

It's a man's world, and I for one wouldn't swap my world for anything.

That old saying; "if you're a woman you have to do things twice as well as men to be considered half as good", couldn't however ring truer. There is only place for whole birds and game girls here if you are not to be treated as a waif who needs looking after, which may be charming, but has a very short shelf-life. Women have always played a major part in field sports, especially game shooting and gun dogs. Whilst my grandmother Mrs Green was legendary in the kitchen, another great lady was legendary with the dogs. Mrs Town was the most respected and talented trainer of field trial champion English Setters in her time. Growing up with these women and their stories in my life, and having a natural affinity for sports and animals, I never considered that I couldn't hold my own amongst the boys.

It was an awfully hot day in September on the grouse moor and I can honestly say I have only twice before felt exhaustion quite like it. Once when riding ten newly backed horses one after the other, the other whilst working out in Tanzania in 50°C. The sweat was stinging my eyes to the point I couldn't actually see, my legs had gone to jelly, and I really didn't know if I wanted to throw up or cry. Somehow though you dig deep and find that other gear. When stopped for lunch, I was asked if I wanted to flank rather than beat for the afternoon. Having been fore-warned that this next drive involved an hour and a half semi-gallop just to line out over almost continuous peat

hags, I was ready with my answer: "no I'm perfectly fine to continue". My god, being the only girl out I couldn't possibly let the side down. Of course this has since back-fired on me, as I don't get asked now, I'm just treated as part of the team.

On pheasants I have at times had to prove my worth picking up, and that girls can train dogs, often going further back for runners than most. Belle, my top dog, is thankfully the best allied force one could wish for. An acquaintance who has always been sceptical of the female race's ability to work gun dogs was struggling to find a bird. He had sent his trusty old Labrador into the gorse bushes several times, and I could see he was starting to huff and puff. He finally relented and asked me to pop Belle in, whilst simultaneously exhorting that the bird couldn't have been hit hard and must have gone on. All went quiet, I knew Belle was busy, and after a few minutes out she came, carrying a huge bird and gently laid it in my hand. I said nothing, just headed down the hill with my prize. Behind I heard voices; "gosh she's not bad, last week she found my cock, and this week she's found yours". This is the point at which all you can do is smile.

At the end of this season on keeper's day I swung 180 degrees through a very high pheasant, and dropped it tumbling out of the sky with my first barrel. At that there was a little round of applause from the three gentlemen leaning on a Landrover behind me, they have quietly watched me over the years. Believe me, success has never tasted so sweet.

Duck on a Date
Served with Buttered Fennel and Classic Roast Potatoes

The duck went on a date with some sozzled clementines, and ended the night being laced with honey. Clementines don't have the pips like oranges and are sweeter, with less acidity. The result is a much more delicate citrus flavour than with most 'duck and orange' dishes. I absolutely love the combination of fennel, potatoes, and bacon. The earthy depth of the dates and fennel is lifted here with the sweet citrus and honey, as not to over-power the duck. Combined with classic roast potatoes, what's not to like.

Serves Two

Ingredients

1 Mallard duck, dressed

1 Red onion

6 Clementines

Brandy, dark rum, or
if you can get hold of
some honey rum
even better

10 Dates

10 Rashers
streaky bacon

Heather honey

Sea salt

Duck fat or extra
virgin olive oil

1kg Potatoes

50g Butter

1 Fennel bulb

For the Duck:

Cut 2 – 3 clementines into 0.5cm horizontal slices, so that the segments don't fall apart. Lay them in a shallow bowl and sprinkle over a tablespoon or two of brandy or dark rum. I discovered honey rum in the Canaries, personally the barren volcanic landscape didn't do a lot for me, but the rum was exceptional! Leave the clementines to soak up your chosen spirit for an hour.

Wrap each date in a slice of streaky bacon, and lay in the bottom of a roasting tin, creating an oval shape for the duck to sit on. Place the peeled and halved red onion in the duck's cavity, and sit it on the dates. Carefully lay the clementine slices all over the duck. Cover with a lid, and roast in a pre-heated oven at 200°C for 40 minutes. Remove the lid from the roasting tin, gently push the clementine slices off the duck, sprinkle a little sea salt over the skin, and return to the top of the oven for 8 - 10 minutes to allow the skin to brown and crisp.

For the Roast Potatoes:

Peel and halve or quarter the potatoes, depending on their size. Place in a large pan of boiling water, and cook for 5 minutes. Drain the potatoes in a colander, giving them a good shake about to slightly 'rough them up'. Add 100mls of duck fat, or if you're not feeling quite that luxurious several generous lugs of extra-virgin olive oil, in a roasting tin and place in the hot oven for 5 minutes. Sprinkle the drained potatoes with a little sea salt, and then pop them in the hot fat. Be careful not to get burnt with splashes when you drop the potatoes in, roll them around to make sure they are well coated with fat on all sides. Return the tin to the oven and roast for 40 minutes until crisp and golden.

For the Buttered Fennel:

Remove the feathery tops, base, and tough outer layer from a bulb of Italian fennel. Slice it into thin wedges. Heat the butter in a saucepan until melted but not colouring, over a moderate heat. Add the fennel wedges and gently cook for 10 minutes in the hot butter, until tender but retaining bite, without letting them brown. You are almost poaching the fennel in butter.

For the Honey Sauce:

Squeeze the juice from 2 or 3 clementines, depending on their size, to equate to about 100mls of liquid. Pour a 30ml shot of your chosen spirit; brandy or dark rum, into a saucepan and bring to the boil. Boil rapidly for a few minutes, to evaporate the harsh alcohol and reduce the volume by half, then add the clementine juice. Bring this briefly to the boil, then reduce to a steady simmer and stir in 2 teaspoons of heather honey. Allow the sauce to continue to simmer gently for another 5 to 10 minutes, until slightly thickened and glossy.

To Serve:

Rest the duck on a board for 10 minutes prior to carving. Serve thin slices of meat, a date or two and a few wedges of fennel, with the roast potatoes, trickling the honey sauce over the meat and vegetables at the end.

A rather fabulous date.

Show Stoppers

Pan-fried Grouse Breast with Stilton, Mushroom and Red Wine Sauce

Served with Home-made Chips and Watercress Salad

*G*rouse have to be my favourite little 'game birds'. They're so wick and can fly hundreds in a pack into a head wind you can hardly stand up in shouting "go back, go back". They don't need a lot of hanging, to avoid that strong smell and taste of peat and heather, which isn't to everyone's liking, I say shot one day, dressed the next. Some believe the meat off young grouse is an aphrodisiac, all I can vouch for is they're delicious, and don't need much, comparable to a superb fillet steak.

Serves Two

Ingredients

The breasts off 2
young grouse

Extra-virgin olive oil

3 – 4 Large potatoes

Himalayan Pink salt

1 Large shallot, peeled
and finely chopped

1 Garlic clove, bruised
and finely chopped

Glass of good red wine
(about 200mls)

300mls Double cream

150g Stilton

200g Baby
button mushrooms

Butter

Watercress

For the Chips:

Peel and cut the potatoes lengthways into chips. Rinse to remove excess starch, pat dry and place in a roasting tray. Add a couple of lugs of extra-virgin olive oil, turn the chips over in the oil with your hands to ensure they are evenly coated, then spread out and sprinkle on some Himalayan Pink salt. Cook in the hot oven, pre-heated to 220ºC for approximately 40 minutes until golden in colour, turning once.

For the Sauce:

To make the sauce gently sauté the shallots and garlic in a little olive oil for about 5 minutes until soft but not brown, in a small, high sided sauce pan. Add the red wine and turn up the heat, allow to boil and reduce by half, which will take approximately another 5 minutes and the smell is fantastic. Once reduced turn the heat right back down and add the double cream. Mix well to get a lovely lilac sauce, then add the crumbled Stilton and allow to simmer very gently for at least 20 minutes. As the sauce cooks and the cheese melts it will thicken, keep an eye on it and stir regularly so it doesn't burn. Quickly fry the mushrooms in a knob of butter and add to the sauce once it has thickened.

For the Grouse:

Place the grouse breasts on a plate and rub a generous lug of extra-virgin olive oil into the meat, massaging it in with your fingers. Now leave to relax at room temperature until ready to cook them (at least half an hour). If you cook the meat from cold the muscle fibres will still be contracted and the meat will be tough.

When the chips and sauce are about ready it's time to cook your grouse. Heat a heavy bottomed frying pan until very hot… fortune favours the brave! Do not add any oil to the pan, the oil is already on the grouse. Lay the grouse breasts in the pan and turn down the heat a little. Press down on each breast with a spatula to make sure all the meat gets the heat. After 2 minutes turn over and cook the other side for another 2 minutes for pink, 3 minutes each side for medium. Remove from the pan and rest, covered with foil to retain heat, for 5 minutes.

To Serve:

Serve two grouse breast per person with the chips, watercress salad and sauce.

A wonderful simple dish that tastes like heaven!

If there's any sauce left over my guilty pleasure is to have it cold the next day, slathered on toast.

A Little Prestige

In 1997 Anne Willan, one of the most authoritative figures in culinary finesse wrote a superb book; Cooked to Perfection, which explains how to get things right in the kitchen, from gravies to cakes. It includes a wonderful recipe for fruit cake: Mrs Green's Christmas Cake. Thankfully my grandmother was still alive to delight in the fact that her recipe had been chosen for the perfect fruit cake. Someone said to me a little out of the blue, almost two decades later; "Oh your grandmother's Christmas Cakes really were the best, so rich yet light". Her recipe book was handed down to me, and I bake it from her hand written instructions, which feels very special every time.

I got my recognition at the CLA Game Fair in 2015, when I cooked in the finals of the amateur section of the Game Chef of the Year, and only narrowly missed out on the top spot. Sadly Mrs Green is no longer with us to have shared my achievement. It is however because of her belief and encouragement that I had the gumption to go and try.

I also inherited the simple fact that I love cooking. I suppose it is a form of art in that you are creating something beautiful from raw materials. It is all about balancing textures and flavours. For me it is also a way to relax, admittedly I find it very easy, but I do get a wonderful sense of achievement. This is especially true when those you cook for are genuinely enjoying what you are serving them, be that your family on a Wednesday evening or a group of friends at a dinner party. Of course, a little prestige gives you that extra sparkle, and the dishes in this section are just that, with my pièce de résistance; Pan-fried Grouse Breast.

Inebriated Pheasant Breasts
Served with Roasted New Potatoes, Wilted Spinach and Field Mushrooms

T his is the very first main course I invented completely from scratch. I must have made it hundreds of times, and it still tastes and looks fabulous. The instruction for using a red wine good enough to drink is very important here, cheap, nasty stuff won't cut the mustard, and as the pheasants are soaked for such a long time there's no hiding from it. If you're going to get inebriated, do it with class.

Serves Four

Ingredients

4 – 8 Pheasant breasts,
depending on the size
of your birds
and appetite

Bottle of red wine
(a nice Malbec or
Bordeaux for example)

8 – 16 Slices of
Parma ham

Baby new potatoes

Extra-virgin olive oil

Small bunch of
rosemary

Zest of 1 lemon

Sea salt

Bag of young
spinach leaves

Nutmeg seed

Demerara sugar

4 Field mushrooms

Butter

2 Shallots

3 Cloves of garlic

For the Pheasant Breasts:

Place the pheasant breasts in a large glass bowl and pour enough red wine over to completely submerge them. Cover the bowl with cling film and refrigerate for at least 10 hours. When I make this I tend to do this bit as soon as I get up on a morning, whilst the kettle is boiling for my first cup of tea of the day.

Remove the bowl from the fridge half an hour before you are ready to cook the meal, to allow everything to come up to room temperature. Take the pheasant breasts from the bowl of wine, shaking off any excess liquid. They will be well and truly inebriated, the meat will have turned a fabulous purple colour, and the wine will have thickened and become paler with the juices released from the meat. Not something you would want to put in a glass, but it's going to make a fantastic jus later on. Wrap each pheasant breast in Parma ham, on average each one will need one and a half slices of ham, but this will depend on the size of the bird. The meat does not need seasoning as the salt from the cured Parma ham will achieve this during cooking. Place the wrapped up pheasant breasts in a shallow roasting tin, and cover with foil. Roast in the centre of a pre-heated oven at 180°C for 40 minutes, removing the foil for the final 10 minutes to allow the outside of the meat to crisp up.

For the Roasted New Potatoes:

Prepare the new potatoes by washing them, but the skins need to stay intact, so do not scrub too exuberantly. Small, baby potatoes are best, I like them so tiny I can pop a whole one in my mouth, like a hot sweet! Heat several generous lugs of extra-virgin olive oil in a roasting tin, by placing it in the pre-heated oven at 180°C until sizzling. Remove the tin from the oven and carefully lay the potatoes in the hot oil as quickly as possible before it cools. Roll them around so they are well coated in oil, then add in the finely grated zest of one lemon, and finely chopped leaves off 2 or 3 sprigs of rosemary, and a generous sprinkling of sea salt. Roll everything around in the tin again to ensure even coating, before returning to the top of the oven for 30 minutes. The result will be a cross between sweet little golden roast and baked potatoes.

For the Field Mushrooms:

De-stalk and free the mushrooms of any dirt by brushing it off. If necessary, carefully peel the outer layer of flesh off, from the rim of the cap down with your fingers. Place the mushrooms, on their backs, cap side down, on a baking tray. Crush and chop 2 cloves of garlic, and divide between the mushrooms, then dot each one with a little knob of butter in the centre where the stalk has been removed. Bake in the bottom of the oven, at 180°C for 30 minutes.

For the Wilted Spinach:

Heat a dry frying pan until hot, place a big handful of rinsed baby spinach leaves in the pan, and fry, moving them almost continuously, for a minute or two until wilted. Transfer the cooked spinach to a warmed bowl and place in the oven to keep warm, repeat until you have used all the leaves. Allow one big handful of fresh leaves per person, it may look like a lot but spinach reduces massively once cooked.

For the Jus:

Chop the shallots and remaining garlic clove. Once the pheasant breasts have cooked place them on a board to rest. Take the roasting tin and place it on your hob over a moderate heat. Add the shallots and garlic and fry until browning, adding a small amount of extra-virgin olive oil to the tin if it is quite dry. Now turn up the heat and pour in the red wine that the pheasants got inebriated in. It will bubble and crackle, lifting all the lovely flavours up. Stirring with a whisk, making sure to scrape the base of the roasting tin, continue to boil the liquid for a few minutes until reduced to a jus.

To Serve:

On each plate place a bed of wilted spinach, scattered with a fresh grating of nutmeg and a pinch of demerara sugar, then lay the pheasant breasts on top. Add a baked field mushroom beside, with a spoonful of shallot jus. I tend to let everyone help themselves to the potatoes, by placing them in a warm bowl in the centre of the table, along with any remaining jus in a jug.

Sublime, especially with a glass or two of your chosen red wine.

Pan-fried Venison Loin with Port, Dark Chocolate, & Damson Reduction

Served with Beetroot Purée and Pommes de Terre Noisette

I entered the 2015 CLA Game Chef of The Year competition (amateur section) on a bit of a whim really. Encouraged by a friend, who realised I was good enough, I was totally stunned to get through to the finals. After much discussion and trials (which no one seemed to mind) this is the dish I cooked on the day, in a marquee, with hundreds of people watching. It came down to a pinch of salt which put me into second place, literarily, but if you are cooking this at home you can season it just how you want.

Serves Two

Ingredients

Loin from a saddle of venison, if using Red Deer half a loin is sufficient, 1 full loin if it's off a little Roe Deer (a full 5kg saddle from a red deer will give you enough to feed 8, a loin off each side, divided into 2)

Rapeseed oil

Freshly ground black pepper

Himalayan Pink salt

4 Medium beetroot

4 Large, waxy, yellow potatoes (try the Choppin variety they are fantastic!)

Butter

150mls Ruby port

2 Teaspoons damson jelly

Very dark chocolate

The potatoes need preparing at least 2 hours in advance, I hear you sigh. But actually all that is required is that you peel and wash them, then place (whole) in a large pan of cold, salted, water. This helps to remove the starch and makes a big difference to the end result.

For the Beetroot:

If you have enough time boil the beetroot whole for approximately 45 minutes until tender. This stops the colour bleeding out and makes them easier to peel as the skin will just rub off with your fingers. If time is limited, peel the beets, and chop into 1 cm square cubes. Then place in boiling water and continue to boil for 15 minutes until tender. However you have cooked the beetroot, once tender and peeled, drain and return to the pan. Using the infamous hand held stick blender, purée being careful not to redecorate the kitchen bright pink! Once smooth, season with salt and a generous pinch or two of black pepper. Remember, taste it, add a little more, taste again. This can now be kept warm in the pan or transferred to an ovenproof dish, covered with foil and placed in the bottom of the oven until needed.

For the Venison:

Massage the loin of venison with a generous lug of rapeseed oil about 30 minutes prior to cooking. Season the meat lightly by rubbing Himalayan pink salt in after the oil. Then let it relax at room temperature.

Once ready to cook, probably after you've got the sauce and potatoes on the go, and the beetroot done, heat a dry, heavy bottomed frying pan to hot. Fortune favours the brave, so don't be cautious, if you hold your hand above the bottom of the pan you should feel the heat radiating up almost immediately, now you know it's ready. Place the venison loin in the pan whole and turn down the heat a little. The aim is to seal all sides of the loin quickly, and take long enough to cook the meat (although this dish should be eaten pink). If the meat sticks to the pan, it's not ready to turn, or you've taking your eye off and it has burnt on! An average loin should take 10 minutes to cook. Then remove from the pan onto a board for resting, and with a very sharp knife cut into the meat to check if it's cooked. It should be a lovely bright pink colour, not look red and dense (that's raw). If you think it needs more, return to the pan, otherwise cover with foil and allow to rest on the board for 10 minutes.

For the Pomme de Terre Noisette:

Remove the soaked potatoes from the water, and using a melon baler take out small balls of raw potato. Heat a large knob of salted butter in a frying pan over a moderate heat until foaming. Then add the potato balls and fry until golden brown on all sides, approximately 8 minutes. Transfer into an oven-proof dish and place in the middle of a warm oven (180ºC) for about 10 minutes, making sure they don't become too brown.

At The Game Fair I had the delight of the option to use a truffle in my dish. All I did was laid a few wafer thin slices in with the potatoes before they went into the oven,

if you too have this option I would highly recommend it!

On stage while I was cooking in the finals there were two things the judges took particular note of: Firstly the pan I was using to cook my venison; it's from a set of old cast iron skillets. They are the epitome of how a frying pan doubles up as a weapon, they are so heavy you would not want a clout over the back of the head with one. My father bought said pans in a 'garage-sale' when we lived in Saudi-Arabia in the 1980's. If you have a similar pan lurking about or find such a gem at a car boot sale, cherish it. They are unequalled for cooking meat this way as the heat is distributed evenly, and give a delicate searing effect.

The other curiosity of note was my chocolate, a solid bullion of almost 100% cacao. To taste on its own it should be bitter, and give you a strange surge of decadence. Kept in the fridge it is very easy to use a vegetable peeler to scrape off small quantities when cooking.

For the Sauce:

Bring the port to the boil, and boil rapidly for a few minutes until reduced by half. Turn the heat right down and dissolve 2 teaspoons of damson jelly into the port. Once the reduction is smooth scrape four large curls of chocolate into the sauce and stir well. Taste and add more chocolate, a scraping at a time, until you are happy. But be careful not to add too much, or it becomes a chocolate sauce.

To Serve:

Spread a generous table spoon of beetroot on the centre of a warm plate. Slice the venison at an angle into 1 cm cuts, and divide between the plates on top of the beetroot purée, then arrange the Pommes de Terre Noisette alongside, and to finish pour a little sauce down the middle of the venison.

A dish fit for a top spot.

Pan-seared Duck Breast on Chestnut & Garlic Purée

Served with Plum and Orange Sauce, Fried New Potatoes and Broccoli

Not everyone is totally happy dressing duck, maybe it's their feet or the layers of fat and down, but you only need the breasts here so do try to use wild duck. When I was little I remember gathering wild, sweet chestnuts with my father and roasting them over the open fire in a special pan. This dish conjures up thoughts of crisp autumn days and the approaching festive season.

Serves Two

Ingredients

2 Duck breasts,
off one mallard

Rapeseed oil

Perfect Yorkshire Salt

300g Whole sweet
chestnuts, fresh, tinned
or vac packed

3 Garlic cloves

40g Butter

Double cream

Freshly ground
black pepper

200mls Red wine

3 Large red plums

2 Heaped teaspoons
fine-cut Seville
marmalade

Light brown sugar

800g New potatoes

Fresh parsley

Tender-stem or purple
sprouting broccoli

For the Chestnut and Garlic Purée:

I love roasting chestnuts, and it's not as difficult as you may think. Wash and dry the chestnuts, then make a slit in the outer shell on the flat side of each one from half way down to the top with a sharp knife. Place on a baking tray and roast in the top of the hot oven, pre-heated to 220°C for 15 minutes or so. They will smell delicious and have split slightly open when ready. When they are in season you really must try this way instead of opening a tin. Take the flesh out of each chestnut while still warm and add to a small saucepan with a little water. If you are using readily prepared chestnut add them directly to the pan with the water. Simmer gently and after 10 minutes add the 3 cloves of very finely chopped garlic. Keep an eye on the pan and just add small quantities of water if it starts looking dry. After 30 minutes the chestnuts will be tender, add the butter and allow to melt into the mixture. Now roughly puree with a hand held blender before beating in a tablespoon of double cream and a few twists of freshly ground black pepper.

For the Duck:

Rub the duck breasts with rapeseed oil (olive oil will over power the meat here; so be careful). Then roll them in a little Perfect Yorkshire Salt. This is something you can buy in a jar ready to go from Steenbergs, but is basically a mix of sea salt, black pepper, thyme, sage, oregano, mint, and parsley. So, I suppose you could make your own, but this is a cheat I really like. Having made sure the meat is well coated, allow to relax at room temperature for at least 30 minutes.

When you're ready to cook the duck, heat a dry, heavy bottomed frying pan to very hot. Gently lay the duck breasts in the pan and seal by cooking for about 2 minutes on each side, no pink should remain on the outside. Place on a baking tray and pop into the top of the oven at 220°C for 10 minutes, keeping an eye that they don't burn. Remove from the oven and lay the breasts on a board, with a very sharp knife slice into one to check how cooked it is. It should be on the red side of pink, but not with blood running. Remember it's going to continue to cook while it rests, cover the meat with foil and let it rest for 10 minutes before serving, no compromises!

For the Sauce:

Pour 200mls of good red wine, a Cotes de Rhone or Bordeaux would work very well with this dish, into a little sauce pan. Heat till bubbling and keep it going pretty hard till reduced by half. Rinse, quarter and de-stone the plums and add to the reduced wine. Simmer until the plums are soft and falling apart. Remove from the heat and rub through a fine sieve back into the pan. Now keep it gently warm and add your marmalade. Stir frequently, and when fully

dissolved taste, if it's a bit tart add light brown sugar, half a teaspoon at a time, until it tastes perfect!

For the Vegetables:

One of the best tips I can give you is that vegetables such as broccoli and cauliflower are best zapped in the microwave! Trim and rinse the stems of broccoli and place in a microwaveable shallow dish. Sprinkle over a little sea salt, cover with cling film and give them 3 minutes on a high heat, just before you are ready to eat. Simple.

Par boil the new potatoes for 10 minutes, until just tender, drain the water and allow to steam dry and cool slightly before halving each one lengthways. Heat a generous lug of rapeseed oil in a shallow frying pan, test the heat by adding a small piece of potato, if it sizzles straight away, the oil is hot enough. Add the potatoes and fry quickly on both sides until golden brown. Transfer into an oven-proof dish, snip over some fresh parsley, and if necessary keep warm in the bottom of the oven.

To Serve:

When the duck has rested sufficiently cut it across ways into 1cm thick slices. Place a good tablespoon of the chestnut puree on each warm plate in an oblong with a sliced duck breast on top. A little of the plum and orange sauce can be poured down the middle of the meat and the rest served in a warm jug. Potatoes and broccoli on the side, and you are ready to eat.

This really is worth the effort, which isn't really that much, the flavours work fantastically together.

Pan-fried Woodcock with Yorkshire Leeks

Served on a potato rösti

Woodcock are mystical, strange little birds, with their darting flight and long beaks. An accomplished shot can be easily be outwitted by their quick manoeuvres, an elusive left and right therefore duly earns you membership of the elite Woodcock Club. As they are migratory birds numbers in the UK vary each season, this year there seemed to be a lot about. I do however agree with the sentiments that they should only be shot if they are to be taken home and eaten. As a teenager I had them as whole roasted birds and really was very disappointed. I feel it is perfectly acceptable to just breast them off as there isn't a lot of meat anywhere else on the bird, addition of my 'Yorkshire Leeks' give a far from disappointing dish.

Serves Two

Ingredients

The breasts off
2 woodcock

Extra-virgin olive oil

Sea Salt

4 Large, waxy potatoes

2 – 3 Leeks

200mls Double cream

80g Wensleydale
Cheese

2 Teaspoons
Dijon mustard

Butter

For the Yorkshire Leeks:

This is my Yorkshire version of leeks in cream sauce. The French revere the woodcock, and as such Dijon mustard is a very fitting ingredient here. You can of course use English mustard, if you want to remain patriotic, but start with just one teaspoon, taste, and add more if you like the sharpness.

First, trim the leeks by removing the base, dark green tops, and outer layer, then wash thoroughly. Slice them as finely as you are able to. In a large heavy bottomed frying pan heat a knob of butter (approx. 20g) along with a lug of extra-virgin olive oil over a moderate heat. Once the fats have melted together add the leeks to the pan, and sauté very gently, trying to avoid them from browning, for 15 minutes. Initially there may look to be a lot in the pan, but as the leeks cook down the volume will reduce. Once they are nice and tender pour the double cream into the pan and combine well with the soft leeks, now crumble in the Wensleydale cheese and stir. Allow the contents of the pan just to start to bubble, then turn the heat down and let the mixture thicken as the cheese melts. Keep stirring, ensuring it doesn't catch, after 5 – 10 minutes add the mustard and combine well. The Yorkshire Leeks can be kept warm in the pan until needed.

For the Potato Rösti:

Wash and peel the potatoes, leaving them whole place in boiling water and boil for 8 minutes. Then drain and cool, before coarsely grating them. If you have used waxy potatoes they probably won't release much moisture, but if they seem too wet at this stage squeeze the grated potato in a clean tea towel, as wet potatoes result in soggy rösti. Grease the inside of two 8cm metal chef's rings (or improvise with a pastry cutters) with butter and pack in the grated potato. Sprinkle the tops and bottoms with a little sea salt, then sit the rösti in a frying pan of bubbling hot butter. Turn during cooking to ensure both sides are crisp and golden brown, and the potato is cooked all the way through, fry the rösti for 10 minutes.

For the Woodcock:

The Yorkshire Leeks are full of flavour and sauce, the woodcock should therefore be treated very simply, similar to young grouse. Place the breasts on a plate and pour over a lug or two of extra-virgin olive oil, then massage it into the meat. Allow the woodcock to sit in the oil for about half an hour before rubbing a little sea salt into the breasts. Heat a dry, heavy bottomed frying pan until very hot, so you can just hold your hand above it for a second, then lay the breasts in the pan, and reduce the heat a touch. Fry the breasts for 4 minutes, turning a couple of times to cook the meat evenly. If the meat sticks to the pan it is not ready to turn yet, it's a few minutes of concentration to act before the meat burns, but not too quick.

To Serve:

Place the woodcock on a board to rest for 5 minutes. On warm plates set a potato rösti per person, and surround with a tablespoon full of Yorkshire Leeks. Slice the pan-fried woodcock breasts and sit them on top of each rösti. I really don't need anything else with this dish, but if you have to only add something very simple such as damson jelly or a few boiled sweet carrots.

Sporting Suppers

Grouse Gnocchi

This dish was inspired by a recent trip to Venice, where I ate gnocchi with a 'meat sauce' in a tiny restaurant hidden away from the tourist throng. It was simple and divine, perfect to recreate with my favourite game birds. I use the meat off old grouse for this, a great way to use them up, but young work just as well. In Italy the pasta and gnocchi dishes are not overwhelmed by wet sauces, just enough thick, rich sauce to balance the carbohydrates. A good quality bought gnocchi is perfectly acceptable, and if you're not a fan of gnocchi try it with pasta, big rigatoni or conchiglie shapes work best.

Serves Two

Ingredients

2 Grouse breasts
(i.e. off 1 bird)

Extra-virgin olive oil

Plain flour

Tin of plum tomatoes

Red wine (something
like a Montepulciano
or Valpolicella)

1 Bay leaf

1½ Teaspoons oregano

1 Shallot

1 Garlic clove

For the Grouse Sauce:

The sauce does take 5 hours in a slow cooker, or you could use an oven-proof dish with a tightly fitting lid at 120°C, however it is well worth the wait. Slice each grouse breast lengthways into 3 and dust the meat on all sides with plain flour. Heat 2 tablespoons of extra-virgin olive oil in a heavy bottomed frying pan until hot. Add the meat and brown on all sides. As soon as the meat is sealed remove it and transfer into the slow cooker. In the same frying pan sweat the finely chopped shallot and garlic over a low heat, until soft. Add these to the grouse in the slow cooker with the bay leaf, oregano, and a small glass (about 150mls) of red wine. As you should only cook with wine which is good enough to drink, I recommend setting the bottle aside to enjoy with supper. Stir the ingredients and set the slow cooker going on high for an hour.

After that first hour add a tin of whole peeled plum tomatoes. Stir them in but try not to break the tomatoes at this stage. Allow to cook away for another 3 hours, occasionally checking that the dish isn't drying out, if so add a splash more red wine. The meat should now be very soft and easily broken up into small flakes with a spoon. Break the tomatoes up too, and stir so it is a lovely rich meaty sauce. The sauce needs another hour slowly bubbling away before you remove the bay leaf and are ready to serve.

For the Gnocchi:

Add the gnocchi or pasta, to a large pan of boiling, salted water. The water must be boiling and salted, a lady in an Italian deli told me this, and yes it does make all the difference. Then cook the gnocchi until it floats to the top of the water which will take approximately 3 minutes, or the pasta for 10 minutes. Do not overcook either, it will become soggy. Drain and toss in a drizzle of extra virgin olive oil.

To Serve:

Serve in big warm bowls; gnocchi, sauce, and a grating of parmesan. With a simple rocket salad drizzled with balsamic syrup, and the rest of that very good bottle of red wine! Bon appétit!

Pheasant & Pea Risotto

*T his is a great way of using up leftover pheasant. If two have had one bird for supper there's usually enough
left on the carcass to make this dish and it tends to be the lovely crumbly white bits from around the wish
bone and darker leg meat that remains which works so well here. If you haven't got leftovers one breast should be
enough for two people. There's something strangely fresh but comforting about this risotto, which means it works
just as well for a girl's lunch in the summer as it does on a cold winter's night in front of the fire.*

Serves Two

Ingredients

Cooked pheasant meat
broken up into slices
and some smaller
pieces

100g Frozen peas

3 Celery sticks

2 Medium shallots

2 Garlic cloves

Extra virgin olive oil

200g Risotto rice

500mls Stock

Sea salt

150mls Crisp dry
white wine

Parmesan or
mascarpone cheese
(or both!)

1 Loaf ciabatta bread
cut into thick slices

For the Risotto:

Heat a good lug of extra-virgin olive oil in a large, high-sided
saucepan. Finely slice the celery, use the lighter, middle sticks,
shallots and garlic, and gently fry in the oil for a few minutes
until starting to soften but not colouring. At the same time
heat your stock in a pan and keep it simmering. Pheasant
stock is preferable, but vegetable is fine. It's even ok to use
some made from a good quality cube, at the end of the day in
the real world people have busy lives and this is a perfectly
acceptable cheat.

Once the vegetables have softened increase the heat under
your pan and add the risotto rice, fry until it starts to look
translucent. This will only take a few minutes and the rice can
easily burn, so keep it moving so it doesn't catch. Then pour
in the wine, it will crackle, that's fine it's supposed to. Keep
stirring until all the wine has cooked into the rice, add a pinch
of sea salt, then turn the heat back down a little to a medium
temperature. Cook risotto rice too quickly and it will stay hard
and chewy, too slowly and you will get exceedingly bored.

Add a cup full or so of hot stock at a time to the risotto, working the liquid into the rice by stirring with a wooden spoon before the next addition of stock. When almost all the stock has been added to the rice, this will take about 30 minutes, taste it for texture, when it's nearly there add the pheasant meat. Continue the process of adding liquid, boiling water can be used if you run out of stock, in small quantities until the correct 'bite' of the rice is achieved. Add the peas, the heat from the risotto will cook them, a lug of extra-virgin olive oil, and stir through.

To Serve:

After a couple more minutes remove the pan from the heat, and spoon the risotto into warmed bowls. Serve with a dessertspoon of mascarpone on top, grated parmesan, or both, and crusty ciabatta. I love a peppery rocket salad on the side, the choice is yours.

Thai Green Pheasant Curry
Served with Flat Breads

S ome people may refer to pheasants as wild chicken as a result of them suiting so many different dishes; from whole roast birds to risottos, stir-fries, curries, and sandwiches. Personally I think each meat should be thought of and respected in their own way, it is certainly not a discredit to the pheasant, but demonstrates its depth of flavour and texture that it can be cooked in such diverse ways. Thai Green Curry has a delicate heat, which is complimented beautifully by addition of the sweet carrots. I like to keep this light by only using the breast meat off hen pheasants, addition of leg meat will however give a more convincing 'gaminess' to the dish.

Serves Four

Ingredients

Meat off 2 pheasants

Plain flour

Rapeseed oil

2 White onions

1 Jar of Thai Green
curry paste

6 Medium sized
thin carrots

1 Tin Coconut milk

Himalayan Pink salt

Black pepper

Fresh Coriander

300g Basmati rice

300g Plain flour

180mls Warm water

1 Teaspoon fine salt

For the Thai Green Curry:

Take the meat you want to use off the pheasants, the remaining carcasses and meat can be used for other dishes such as the Pheasant and Pea Risotto or made into stock. Slice the pheasant meat into strips, and dust them generously with plain flour. Heat a lug of rapeseed oil in a heavy bottomed frying pan over a high heat, add the pheasant strips to the pan and quickly fry them on all sides, to seal and brown the meat, then remove from the pan and set to one side on a plate lined with absorbent paper.

Peel and finely slice the onions, then peel the carrots and cut them into batons about 0.5cm thick and 5cm long. In a wok or large frying pan with high sides, heat a lug of rapeseed oil over a moderate temperature and sauté the onions for 5 minutes until soft. Empty a jar of Thai Green curry paste into the pan and stir-fry with the onions for a further 3 minutes before adding in the carrot batons and pheasant strips, continue to cook and stir so that all the elements are coated in curry paste. Open the tin of coconut milk and scrape this out into a bowl, coconut milk usually separates in the tin so give it a good stir to reconstitute it before adding to the curry. Mix all the elements together in the pan, cover with a lid and allow to simmer for 30 minutes before serving. Stir every so often to prevent the curry catching on the bottom of the pan, and add a little splash of water if it looks too dry.

For the Flat Breads:

In a mixing bowl combine the flour and salt, then mix the lukewarm water and a tablespoon of rapeseed oil in a jug and pour this into the flour whilst stirring with a wooden spoon, continue to stir until it all comes together. Knead the dough and once it feels elastic and smooth allow it to rest for an hour in the bowl covered with cling film. Unlike conventional bread, this dough will not rise as it doesn't contain yeast, it just needs to relax.

Cut the dough into eight equal portions, and on a floured surface roll each one into a flat circular shape only 1 or 2mm thick. Heat a dry frying pan and lay the dough in, you will see it change colour and texture as it cooks, just like a pancake does. Flip the flat bread over and cook the other side for a minute or so until set, then remove from the pan and repeat with the other seven pieces. Do not worry if the breads puff up a little whilst cooking, and any charred bits add flavour.

The cooked breads can be kept warm wrapped in a clean tea towel. I like to have at least 2 pans on the go with the flat breads, so that they are cooked quickly and served fresh.

For the Basmati Rice:

Check the packet instructions for the basmati rice. Usually cooking this quantity of rice involves adding it to 1500mls of boiling water with half a teaspoon of salt, continue to boil for 10 minutes, then drain.

To Serve:

Plate up a portion of the rice with Thai Green pheasant curry for each person, sprinkle fresh coriander leaves on top and let everyone help themselves to the flat breads from the middle of the table.

A personal recommendation from those who have tested these recipes out, my long suffering friends, is to have the Venison and Beansprout Spring Rolls as a starter, and the Heather Honey and Cardamom Ice Cream as dessert with this dish for a real feast.

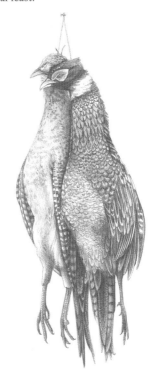

Pheasant Stir-fry

S amphire is a sea vegetable which grows naturally along the southern coast of the UK, it was harvested by hand for many centuries. Whilst very popular in Elizabethan England, it has only recently gained popularity in modern times and can now easily be bought from the vegetable aisle in most supermarkets. The salty taste really compliments the pheasant, without drying it too much due to the quick cooking nature of this dish. I have never quite understood the need to add a packet of sauce into stir-fries, the meat, vegetables, soy sauce, and oil give enough flavour which would be overwhelmed and their identity lost if you added anything else.

Serves Four

Ingredients

2 Pheasant breasts

Stir-fry oil

1 White onion

2 Garlic cloves

1 Red and
1 yellow pepper

150g mushrooms

100g Samphire

Dark soy sauce

Fine egg noodles

For the Stir Fry:

Slice the onion finely, and chop the garlic. Prepare the mushrooms and peppers by cutting them into slices, as fine or chunky as you like, and wash the samphire. On a separate board cut the pheasant into pieces a similar size to the peppers. In a wok or large frying pan heat a lug of stir-fry oil over a moderate heat. If you do not have any stir-fry oil use rapeseed oil, adding a little grated fresh ginger and an extra garlic clove in with the onions. Add the onion and garlic and sauté for five minutes, until the vegetables are tender and just starting to colour. Turn up the temperature, and once the pan is hot add the pheasant pieces and stir fry them quickly browning on all sides, then add the soy sauce. Once the pheasant has been sealed and coloured the heat can be turned down a little before adding the peppers and mushrooms to the mix. Cook for another 10 minutes, stirring frequently; hence the name stir-fry, during this time cook your noodles and warm the bowls. For the last 3 minutes add the samphire into the pan. Both samphire and soy sauce bring salt to the dish, therefore you do not need to add any extra seasoning during cooking, do taste the stir-fry and add a little more soy sauce if required.

For the Noodles:

Bring a large pan of water to the boil, allowing one nest of noodles per person place them in the boiling water and continue to cook for 3 minutes, unless the packet instructions tell you otherwise.

To Serve:

Split the drained noodles between four warmed bowls, and pile the stir-fry on top, ensuring everyone gets a fair share of vegetables and meat. Some crunchy prawn crackers on the side won't go amiss either.

Pheasant au Fromage

The key to success for this dish is if you know your cock from your hen birds! If you have read the indispensable knowledge and understanding in the first section of this book you will appreciate the importance of the difference in the flavour and texture of the meat. Cock birds have a robust meat and strong flavour, capable of taking a ripe brie or nutty mature cheddar, and smoked bacon. Whilst the delicate meat off hen birds needs something like a light Wensleydale or young Vignotte, with unsmoked bacon. It always makes me giggle when I go into the game dealer's and they radio through to the back; "Esther is here to collect her 26 cocks!" no-one else bats an eyelid, but I do think it's important to keep a light sense of humour.

Serves Two

Ingredients

4 Pheasant breast
(off hen or cock
birds, don't get them
muddled up)

4 Slices of bacon
(smoked or un-smoked,
as appropriate for the
chosen pheasant)

8 generous slices of
suitable cheese

For the Pheasant:

With a sharp knife slit the side of each breast lengthways, not quite all the way through though. Place slices of your chosen cheese in between the meat, and then secure by wrapping each breast in a slice of the corresponding bacon, dependant on the bird. The salt from the bacon will season the pheasant as it cooks. Place the breasts side by side on a baking tray in the middle of the oven, pre-heated to 180°C and bake for 35 minutes.

To Serve:

Serve with seasonal vegetables and boiled potatoes, salad and fried new potatoes, or even more lovely and easy a tin of sweetcorn and chips!

Rabbit Curry, Mathikere Style
Served with Basmati Rice and Cooling Yogurt

Serves Four

Ingredients

600g of rabbit meat, equivalent to the haunches and loins of 3 rabbits

Rapeseed oil

2 White onions

1 Teaspoon Turmeric powder

1 Teaspoon chilli powder

1 Teaspoon salt

½ Garlic bulb

3cm Piece of fresh root ginger

2 Tablespoons Tahini

3 Tablespoons desiccated coconut

2 Tomatoes

1 Tablespoon coriander powder

1 Teaspoon Garam Masala powder

2 Tablespoons fresh coriander leaves

Fresh green chilli

300g Basmati rice

300ml Natural yogurt

Sea salt

Small handful fresh mint and coriander leaves

1 Lime

This curry was inspired by an Indian girl who taught me how to make Garam Masala from scratch. She gave me the idea for this dish from one of her family's recipes, which I have adapted to suit rabbit and made it a little more user friendly to the average country kitchen, without losing the essence of India. Rabbit is ideal for curry as the strong texture of the meat can stand up to the robust spices and cooking methods, while its delicate flavour does not try to compete with the seasoning.

For the Curry:

I find making Garam Masala from scratch very satisfying, and love working with all the different spices, however it really is beyond the remit of this book as you can buy very good ready-made powder in the spice aisle of any supermarket.

First prepare the garlic-ginger paste by peeling the cloves from half a decent sized bulb of garlic. This may seem a lot, but trust me it works. Then peel the piece of ginger and chop it up. Combine the garlic and ginger by making it into a paste by blitzing in a spice grinder or bashing up with an old fashioned pestle and mortar.

Ideally in a large wok, otherwise a high sided frying pan heat a good lug or two of rapeseed oil over a moderately high temperature. Chop the onion very finely and add to the pan, fry until tender and light golden brown. Then add the rabbit meat which should be diced into bite sized pieces, with the Turmeric powder, chilli powder, and a teaspoon of fine sea salt. Fry these together for a few minutes until the meat is sealed and browned on all sides, before turning down the heat and adding 2 teaspoons of garlic-ginger paste to the pan, and continue to cook.

In a separate pan dry fry the Garam Masala powder, coriander powder and desiccated coconut for a minute or two, just enough to release their aromas fully. Then add a little rapeseed oil and once this has heated up add the second finely chopped onion and quartered tomatoes. After a few more minutes, once these ingredients are starting to soften add the Tahini and fresh coriander to the pan and combine thoroughly. Scrape the mixture into a bowl and blend into a fine sauce with a stick blender.

Add the sauce to the pan containing the rabbit and fold in thoroughly, continue to simmer the curry for 30 minutes until the meat is tender. If it looks a little dry simply add a splash of water to loosen it.

For the Rice:

Cook the basmati rice according to the instructions on the packet, this usually involves adding the basmati rice to a large pan of boiling water and boiling for 10 minutes before draining. Advice is to use a good quality rice and not to overcook it. If it's ready before the rest of the dish simply transfer to an ovenproof bowl and cover with a lid to keep warm.

For the Cooling Yogurt:

Cooling yogurt is a great accompaniment to curry, as dairy products helps to make hot curries more palatable. Pour the yogurt into a bowl, add a pinch of sea salt, the juice of half a lime, and finely chopped mint and coriander leaves, mix well and refrigerate until needed.

To Serve:

De-seed and finely slice the green chilli, sprinkle it on top of the rabbit curry. You could plate up a portion of rice and curry for each person, or simply place each element in separate warm serving bowls in the centre of the table and let people help themselves. The addition of a pile of warm flat breads (see page 91) works very well with this curry too.

Bambi on the Pull

Served as part of a Barbeque or with Pitta Breads and Salad

This is my good friend Tad's recipe (her real name is Evelyn but I don't think I've ever heard her called that). She kindly let me include it, the only part I can take credit for is the title, which we all agree is rather apt. Tad and I first met when hunting with neighbouring packs in the pre-ban heydays. She whipped in to the Hurworth Hounds, one of the few females to fulfil this role in a professional capacity. An annoying piece of legislation, marriage to a farmer, children, and age have somewhat steadied our hunting days recently, but we remain close friends. Tad first made this dish for her children's joint birthday party on a hot summer's day, with a piece of venison her parents had brought up from their farm in Wiltshire. It is now a firm favourite, and I urge you to try it.

Serves at least Ten people

Ingredients

3 kg Haunch of
venison, de-boned
and butterflied

40g Butter

1 Onion

5 Garlic cloves

60g Light brown sugar

250ml Tomato ketchup

1 Tablespoon
Worcestershire sauce

2 Tablespoons
dried oregano

1 Tablespoon
Thyme leaves

1 Tablespoon
smoked paprika

120ml Water

250ml Cider vinegar

Sea Salt

Black Pepper

For the Barbeque Sauce:

Place the butter in a saucepan and melt over a moderate heat. Peel and finely chop the onion and garlic cloves, then add to the foaming butter and sauté for about 5 minutes, until soft and starting to turn brown. Add all the other ingredients to the pan in the order listed, it is important to add the cider vinegar last before seasoning with a generous pinch of salt and a couple of good twists of black pepper. Stir well ensuring the sauce is combined, then bring to the boil, just for a moment, before reducing the heat and allowing it to simmer for 20 minutes, stirring frequently. Remove the pan from the heat and allow the sauce to cool completely. Once cool whizz it up in a blender so you get a smooth sauce.

For the Venison:

De-bone and butterfly the haunch of venison if not already done. Tad's knife skills are pretty immense as a result of her previous career, if yours are not that strong get your butcher or game dealer to de-bone the meat for you to save time and making a mess, as the piece of meat does need to stay intact. Take a large roasting tin and place two pieces of tin foil in opposite directions in the tin, making sure the middle of each piece is in the actual tin. Then place the haunch of venison in the tin and smother completely with the cold barbeque sauce. Roll your sleeves up and really get stuck in, making sure it get into every little nook and cranny. Once you are satisfied that the sauce is thoroughly massaged into the meat, wrap it up with the ends of foil, just like a parcel, try to fasten it by folding them together but so that the top of the foil does not touch the meat, otherwise the sauce will stick and possibly burn the foil onto the meat. Place the haunch in the bottom of a pre-heated oven to 120°C and bake for 4 hours. Every so often carefully open the foil and baste the meat in the barbeque sauce, making sure you close the parcel again securely before returning it to the oven. Check that the haunch is done by opening a corner of the foil, the meat should fall away beautifully if pulled at with a fork. Remove from the oven, take it to the barbeque, unwrap and place directly onto the barbeque. It will get lovely and sticky, with gorgeous charred bits. Keep turning the meat until all sides are done. Then place on a board and nominate a willing volunteer to pull it all apart with two forks.

Place the pulled bambi on a big serving platter as part of a barbeque feast, or serve it with pitta breads, fresh salad, and maybe the couscous stolen from the partridge recipe in this book.

To Serve:

Place the pulled bambi on a big serving platter as part of a barbeque feast, or serve it with pitta breads, fresh salad, and maybe the couscous stolen from the partridge recipe (page 126).

A perfect pull!

Venison Cutlets & Black Cherry Sauce
Served with Potato and Celeriac Gratin

hese venison cutlets are gorgeous just on their own, but the sticky black cherry sauce and sumptuous gratin make them really decadent. We've eaten these just with fingers and a knife almost straight off the barbeque while having our regular farm meetings, which usually involves getting straight essential jobs that need doing, feed rations, bills to be paid, followed by lengthy discussions of long term plans and dreams.

Serves Two

Ingredients

2 – 4 Venison cutlets, depending on size and appetite

Extra-virgin olive oil

Dried Oregano

Coarse sea salt

100g Black cherries, de-stalked, halved and stoned

10g Unsalted butter

Light brown sugar

4 Large waxy, yellow potatoes (such as the superb Chopin variety)

1 Celeriac

200mls Double cream

Freshly ground black pepper

100g Parmesan

For the Venison Cutlets:

Ask your butcher or game dealer to cut the size of cutlets you require from a rack of venison. The meat should be lovely and dark with a nice layer of fat along the bone. In a bowl mix 2 tablespoons of extra-virgin olive oil with half a teaspoon of coarse sea salt and 2 teaspoons of dried oregano. Place the cutlets in a shallow dish and rub the seasoned oil all over them, then allow to relax for an hour or so. The cutlets can be either barbequed, grilled or cooked on a griddle pan with a moderate heat for 20-35 minutes, turning every so often to ensure even cooking and making sure both sides are nicely coloured.

For the Potato and Celeriac Gratin:

Peel the celeriac then sit it upright on a board and quarter it. Cut each quarter into slices approximately 0.8cm thick. Peel the potatoes and cut into similar thickness slices as the celeriac. Layer into an oven-proof dish adding a little freshly ground salt and black pepper in between; celeriac, potatoes, celeriac, then a last layer of potatoes but only around the outside, leaving a central lower circle of celeriac exposed. Pour the double cream all over the gratin, making sure it's evenly coated from above. Finish by filling the central delve with grated parmesan and a light sprinkling around the outer potatoes. Cover and place in the oven, pre-heated to 200°C, for 45 minutes, remove the lid from the gratin for the last 15 minutes to allow the top to become crunchy and golden.

For the Black Cherry Sauce:

Place the washed and prepared cherries in a saucepan with 50mls of water and bring slowly to the boil. Gently simmer until the fruit has softened, which will take 10 – 15 minutes. Then add a tablespoon of soft light brown sugar and 50mls of hot water, continue to simmer until the sugar has dissolved. If the liquid still looks thin, increase the heat and boil hard for a few minutes until reduced and thickened, don't leave it at this stage and keep stirring as it can suddenly dry out and burn to the bottom of the pan; not a good look! Now rub the sauce through a fine sieve, discarding the cherry pulp and return the liquid to the saucepan. Add 10g of unsalted butter and melt into the sauce stirring well, over a low heat. Taste and add more sugar if required. The resulting sauce should be dark and glossy.

To Serve:

If going for the rustic look, place the venison cutlets on a board in the centre of the table with the black cherry sauce in a little bowl beside, with a spoon in the gratin and let everyone get stuck in.

For more formal occasions plate up individually, and you may wish to add another vegetable such as crisp green beans. Whatever the circumstances just enjoy this lovely indulgent food.

Goose Stew
Served with Mashed Potato

*A*t the end of the season I have the enjoyment of shooting on Keeper's Day rather than my usual picking up duties, on a little private shoot I have been going to for years. We are all very good friends, someone who has been invited to shoot one week may well be back beating the next. We were stood in total silence, tight in against the wood on the duck drive. An odd unattainable Teal had darted high up above, but all was quiet. Then the silence was broken as geese started to come over, and they just kept coming and coming, the sky was filled with them. What fun, and little Cocker spaniels retrieving enormous Grey Lags from acres of plough is quite a sight! This stew can be made with any variety of goose, but the wild ones will be the tastiest, and really benefit from slow cooking.

Serves Four

Ingredients

Breast off a goose
(i.e. two breasts off
one bird)

Plain flour

Sea salt

Black pepper

Extra-virgin olive oil

2 Red onions

4 Rosemary Sprigs

2 Tablespoons
strawberry or seedless
raspberry jam

½ Butternut squash

3 Carrots

1kg Potatoes

Milk

Butter

For the Goose Stew:

It is amazing how rich and dark goose meat is, almost comparable to beef. Trim any sinew and fat off the meat, then cut it into 2 – 3cm cubes. Place a couple of tablespoons of plain flour in a shallow bowl and season well with sea salt and freshly ground black pepper. In a heavy bottomed frying pan heat a generous lug of extra-virgin olive oil over a high heat, dust each cube of goose meat in the seasoned flour before adding to the pan. Brown the meat on all sides, then transfer to a slow cooker or casserole pan. Peel the onions and cut each one into eight, add to the slow cooking device along with the sprigs of rosemary and about 100mls of boiling water. If you are using an electronic slow cooker set this to high, if using a casserole pan use a low to moderate heat, in both cases make sure the lid is in place to retain heat and moisture. Cook for one hour, then add in the jam. Jam which has set too hard to spread on toast is perfectly fine to use in sauces and stews as the heat dissolves the sugar. Stir it in well and replace the lid, allowing the stew to cook steadily for another hour.

Now it is time to add the vegetables, peel the butternut squash and carrots and chop into similar sized pieces as the goose (2 – 3cm). Add these to the stew and stir well to distribute evenly. Keeping an eye on the heat and liquid level, you can always adjust the temperature, as you want it to cook steadily, and simply add more hot water if it looks a bit dry, cook for a further 3 – 4 hours, so the meat will just fall apart when ready. The beauty of slow cooking things is that timing is not an exact science, allowing plenty of opportunity for late arrivals.

For the Mashed Potato:

Most people can make pretty decent mash, and everyone has their favourite way. Please make it how you like it. This is my favourite way: Peel the potatoes, and halve or quarter them depending on size. Add to boiling water and cook for 20 – 30 minutes until tender. Drain in a colander and steam dry, before returning to the hot pan. Pour in a splash of milk and add approximately 50g of butter, then mash until smooth and season with sea salt and freshly ground black pepper.

To Serve:

Just before you are ready to eat check the consistency and seasoning of the stew, add more salt and pepper as required, remove the rosemary twigs, the leaves will have fallen off. If the gravy needs thickening add a little plain flour to the pot and stir well until cooked in. Serve a generous portion of mashed potato with the goose stew spooned on top.

Perfect for a cold winter's night, especially when you're not quite sure what time supper is required.

Belle

Because Sometimes a Mixture Works Best

I'm really not a fan of mixed dog breeds, dressed up as an extraordinary new dog that we must pay through the nose for. Jackashitz and Cockapoos! Whatever next on a shoot day!

I have a Collie x probably Labrador, we know her mum was a collie because she came off a farm, the father was never seen, but definitely very happy.......as both bitches had pups at the same time. She cost me £60 from the Dog's Trust. She is my best friend, an incredibly special person who knows me better than myself, and at 13 years old has been out beating, on hound exercise, and still helps to gather sheep. However she is not a highly honed working dog who I rely on to do a full day Picking Up.

Now I'm going to completely turn that around and be accused of being an utter hypocrite; because there's Belle. When someone asked me when she was about 6 months old; "what's that?" my answer was simply; "it's Belle". Every time I'm on a shoot in new company I can sense people watching her, before some poor sod gets the privilege of admitting his complete ignorance asking what breed she is; of course she must be a 'breed' to work like that! Usually some kind of foreign Setter or Pointer is suggested. In actual fact, her mother is a little Field Trial bred Springer Spaniel, who I saved from being shot for being timid; she went on to be a truly wonderful gundog for a chap working her on grouse. The father was a German Wired Haired Pointer x Springer Spaniel, who got his wicked way totally by accident, so in actual fact Belle is ¾ Springer ¼ Pointer.

Pike Law is more than 2,000 feet above sea level and some of the hardest terrain on Raby Estate's grouse moors. On the way back down after a superb day, one of the drivers stopped his mule and the two guns in the back kindly offered me a lift. I was about done, so I accepted the opportunity to let my legs stop, Belle and I hopped in. Further down the track we acquired another chap who had been shooting. After parking his 10,000 acre breeks next to me, he scoffed at Belle, who was tucked in on my feet, and proclaimed the obligatory; "what's that". I stupidly explained she was a Springer cross Pointer, which was met by "oh it's a mongrel" and the new passenger promptly turned his back to us. Had I been quick enough I should have replied simply that she is a Springointer and as well-bred as anything else on this truck. If it wasn't for Belle and the likes he would still have been waiting for grouse to fly over, and had a hard search amongst the heather for fallen birds.

What Belle really is;
is absolutely bloody amazing.

She has unrivalled stamina and speed, but control not to over-run her nose. Only a few weeks ago there was a strong runner which she hunted for a good half mile before retrieving the hen bird out of beck. She remained completely focused, needing very little encouragement or direction, her nose barely leaving the ground. I could tell you stories all day about how she has found birds that none of the other dogs could, or how when you think she's spent on a hot August day, she digs deep to find another gear.

She doesn't really play, just hunts, head down, looking for birds. What makes this dog special however is that she so tuned into me. Unbelievably loyal, I have no doubt she would defend me to the end. Crammed into the beater's truck she always sits with her head on me, eye-balling anyone she believes is just a little too close. One blow of the whistle and she is back, approaching at full speed the back legs start to bring her round, so arrival is bottom on my feet looking up at me with eyes that enthuse "what next mummy?!"

That's why, on rare occasions if you combine the best of both you sometimes get something which not only does a job, but has a little bit of the extraordinary; like Belle, or a good game pie.

Game Pie

Served with whatever you fancy

Just like Belle this Game Pie is when a combination produces the best. There is only one rule which you must remember: for every light meat you must add a dark meat. The basic recipe is for pheasant (light) and venison (dark). Should you wish to add in another dark meat, say grouse, then you must add a light one in, for example partridge. It's not rocket science, but it is the difference between a great and mediocre pie.

Serves Four

Ingredients

Shortcrust pastry
(see page 14)

Venison

Pheasant

Bottle of good, full
bodied red wine

Extra-virgin olive oil

2 Bay leaves

Juniper berries or an
orange (optional)

Himalayan Pink Salt

Freshly ground
black pepper

Sage

Mushrooms

Shallots

Butter

Stock

The cut of venison for game pie should have a bone in it, haunch, foreleg, neck or the remains of a saddle (out of which the loins have been taken) are ideal. Cooking the meat with the bone in allows gelatine to seep into the meat giving it a substantial texture which holds better and avoids the need to add things like sausage meat, which for me defeats the purpose of 'game' pie.

Quantities depend on how many you are cooking for, if you have too much meat simply make more pastry and so more pies as they freeze very well.

To give you an idea:

A small foreleg off a Roe deer needs 1 pheasant, 2 large shallots, 300g of mushrooms, and a small bunch of sage leaves, and a double quantity of shortcrust pastry; this will generously cater for 8.

A 3kg haunch of venison (bone in) and 8 pheasant breasts (4 birds) will feed 35 people adequately, just increase the other ingredients accordingly.

The Venison:

This recipe lends very well to using up left overs of venison, but if you are cooking the meat from scratch it must be marinated and slow cooked first, this takes time and sounds a phaf, but trust me it's worth it.

Place the joint of venison into a roasting tin which it fits comfortably. Score the meat with a sharp knife and pour over enough red wine to leave approximately 1cm of liquid in the bottom of the tin. Now rub a little extra-virgin olive oil into the meat. You can add juniper berries, a quartered orange or a pinch of chilli flakes, whatever you fancy really along with the bay leaves. Cover with a tightly fitting lid or foil and allow to marinate in the fridge for at least 6, but up to 12 hours.

When ready to cook the venison remove from the fridge and let it come up to room temperature whilst the oven is heated to

120°C. Baste the meat in the red wine juice out of the bottom of the tin, rub with a little salt and pepper, and place in the oven, covered for about 10 hours.

Check up on the venison every few hours and re-baste with the red wine and meat juice. If it is starting to dry out add a little stock to the tin. The meat is ready when it falls softly off the bone with a fork. When this stage is achieved, remove the lid off the venison and let it have 10 minutes at the top of the oven to crisp up the outside.

The Pheasants:

The pheasant can be roasted very simply, at 180°C. If using whole birds place a peeled shallot in the cavity.

Rub the flesh with a little salt and cover the meat with butter wrappers, roast for 40 minutes. Again allow the meat to have 10 minutes uncovered, at the top of the oven to brown slightly. Pheasant breasts only need 25 minutes covered with butter papers on a baking tray.

The Vegetables:

Chop the mushrooms and fry briskly in olive oil over a moderate heat, cook them in several batches if necessary. In a separate pan melt a generous knob of butter until foaming and sauté the finely sliced shallots until translucent but not browning.

The Jus:

To make the jus, sieve out the bay leaf etc. from the liquid remaining in the venison roasting tin, it can be passed through a fine sieve if necessary and into a clean saucepan. Combine with any liquid from the pheasant, and add stock if you need to bulk it out. Now boil rapidly until reduced and if it needs thickening add half a teaspoon cornflour (or dare I suggest gravy granules). I always add a few scrapings of dark chocolate, it is the little bit of magic that makes the pies special. It is also perfectly acceptable to add in any sauce or

gravy that you have left from a previous meal, such as the Garlicky Maple Pheasant or Port, Dark Chocolate and Damson Reduction, just not anything with cream! The ensuing jus should be the consistency of melted butter.

Assembling the Pies:

Once the meats have cooled enough to handle break the venison into small pieces / flakes and place in a bowl, with the mushrooms and sliced sage. Slice the pheasant into strips, bigger than the venison, and combine with the buttery shallots in a separate bowl. Pour the jus into the venison mixture and then add in the pheasant. Fold it all together so the ingredients are evenly distributed and coated in sauce.

Prepare an appropriate quantity of shortcrust pastry, making sure it has rested in the fridge for at least 30 minutes before you need it. Your chosen pie dishes (or you could use a Yorkshire pudding tin to make individual pies, I did this for a 'drinks' party one Christmas and they went down a storm!) should be lightly dusted with plain flour to prevent the pastry from sticking.

Roll out the pastry to approximately 3mm thickness and line your dishes, allowing the pastry to hang over the edges. Spoon the game into the pies until ¾ full. Brush the edges of the pastry with milk, and cover each dish with pastry and seal the edges by pressing them together with your little finger. The milk helps to seal the pastry, and the tops of the pies should also be brushed with it to help them brown nicely. Bake in a fairly hot oven pre-heated to 200°C for 30 minutes, until the pastry is cooked.

To Serve:

Enjoy with whatever you fancy; chips and peas, roasted vegetables and mashed potatoes, or allow to go cold and pop one in your bait box!

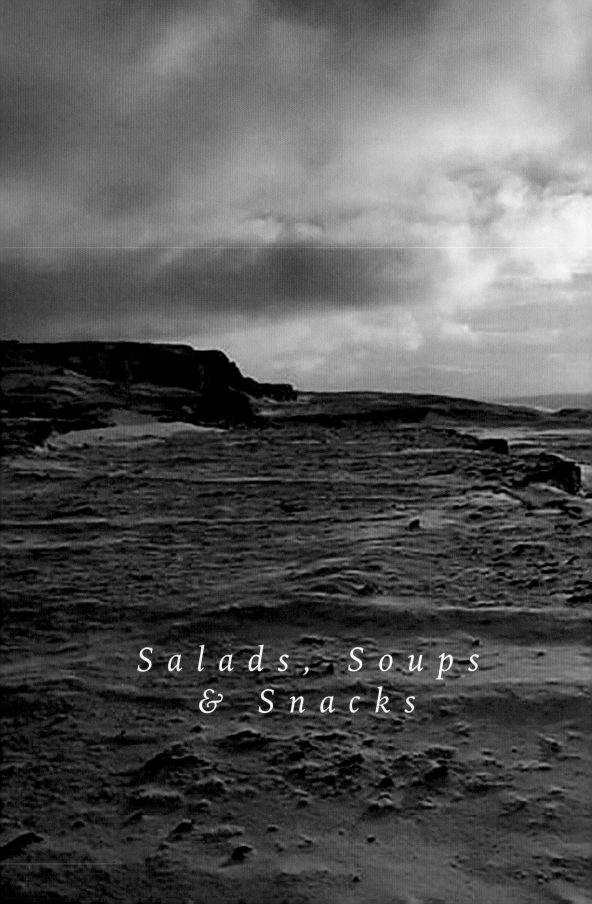

Salads, Soups
& Snacks

Goats' Cheese, Fig, Chorizo, & Heather Honey Salad

*A*lthough this dish does not contain any game, it does utilise honey from the moor. Heather honey has a distinct flavour, which compliments the delicate figs and goat's cheese perfectly. The honey tastes so clean and clear with the fragrance of blooming heather and the wind, it really doesn't compare to anything else. Unless you can buy direct from a small producer you may not be able to get hold of branded 'Heather Honey', as the bees producing it may have had access to other flowers as well as the stunning purple vegetation which provides essential habitat for grouse, so look out for moorland honey. The process of burning heather conducted by game keepers is essential in managing this habitat, as the birds need young plants to feed on and old longer areas to hide and nest in. Through burning, essential minerals retained in the ash are returned to the soil as a natural fertilizer to support regrowth of the young plants.

Serves Two

Ingredients

2 Figs

½ a Link of
Chorizo Sausage

1 Small Chèvre (goats'
cheese, young and light
in colour and texture)

Rocket Leaves

Heather Honey

Extra-virgin olive Oil

Place a handful of rocket leaves in each bowl as a base. Cut the figs into 8 after removing the stalk from the top of the fruit, and arrange on top of the leaves. Now crumble the goats' cheese and divide between the two bowls.

After carefully removing the outer skin, chop the chorizo sausage and fry quickly until golden brown in a hot pan. Only a small amount of olive oil is required as the sausage contains fat which will dissolve out into the pan. Be careful not to fry it for too long as you will lose some of the paprika flavour with the fat. It just wants to be crispy to compliment the soft cheese. Sprinkle on top of the salad, and finish the dish off with a trickle of honey in a criss-cross pattern to ensure you get a little with every mouthful.

Stilton Stuffed Field Mushrooms

T he field mushrooms qualify this dish for inclusion. There is also the sentimental reason that my father loved foraging for fungi, and spent hours learning to identify the edible varieties. I do not profess to be an expert, or even capable of recognising self-picked 'safe' mushrooms, and rely therefore on the source of my local fruit and vegetable supplier. Be warned however; proper field mushrooms are big, flat, and very 'meaty', as such this is a substantial snack or lunch.

Serves Four

Ingredients

4 Field mushrooms

160g Stilton

8 – 12 Slices
Parma Ham

Rocket or
watercress salad

For the Mushrooms:

De-stalk each of the mushrooms and remove any dirt, or if the outsides are damaged peel by gently removing the outer layer of flesh from the edge of the cap to the centre with your fingers. Lay each mushroom on a slice of Parma ham, cap side down, with the gills and area where the stalk was showing. Cut the stilton into slices 0.5cm thick and fill the centres of the mushrooms with cheese. If you are not a fan of stilton it can be replaced with another favoured cheese, nothing too runny however as it won't hold during cooking. Fold the edges of the ham up onto the mushroom, and lay another slice the opposite way over the top of the cheese. Use as much Parma ham as you need to create a parcel enclosing each stuffed mushroom. Once all the mushrooms have been wrapped up lay them in a shallow roasting tin and cover with tinfoil. Bake in a pre-heated oven at 180°C for 30 minutes, then remove the foil. Return to the oven for another 10 minutes to allow the Parma ham to crisp up.

To Serve:

Serve one mushroom per person, with a simple salad such as rocket or watercress leaves on the side. If there are cheesy juices in the roasting tin pour these over the mushrooms once they are plated up, and add some crusty bread to mop up the juices. Scrumptious!

Chilli Honeyed Barbequed Pheasants

*T*here are always pheasant breasts in my freezer, even in the middle of summer. This makes a great addition to any barbeque, whether it is a large party or just two of you enjoying al fresco dining to make the most of a little sunshine!

Serves Four

Ingredients

4 Pheasant breasts

1 Tablespoon extra-virgin olive oil

1 Tablespoon white wine vinegar

2 Tablespoons runny honey

1 Teaspoon dried chilli flakes

Zest of 1 lemon

A generous few pinches of Pink Himalayan salt

For the Pheasants:

Allow one pheasant breast per person, but more if you are only having this with say salad and new potatoes. If you still have a choice at this stage in the year of hen or cock birds, opt for the cock birds for a more robust result. Hen pheasant breasts will work, but be very careful not to overcook them.

In a bowl large enough to take all the pheasant you need, combine the marinade ingredients; oil, vinegar, honey, chilli flakes, finely grated lemon zest, and salt. You are in control, so if you are not a fan of things which are too hot reduce the amount of chilli flakes a little. Similarly use a variety of honey which you like, something mild like oil seed rape flower honey will be much more subtle than heather honey. Whisk the ingredients together by hand until they are thoroughly mixed, then lay the pheasant breasts in the bowl, making sure each one is well coated and submerged before addition of the next piece of meat. Allow the meat to marinade for at least 2 hours before cooking them on the barbeque, for 15 to 20 minutes over a moderate heat.

To Serve:

Check the pheasant breasts are cooked all the way through before serving. These really compliment the Butter Roasted Partridges and Herby Couscous Salad (page 126) and Bambi on the Pull (page 100). Alternatively enjoy them with a simple fresh green salad, some little boiled new potatoes and a glass of something bubbly or a crisp lager.

Pheasant Sandwiches

I went to agricultural college at the tender age of 16. During my two years there I learnt an awful lot more about life, than horses or business. Regularly I would go home at the weekend for some comfort and to be fed properly. As I couldn't drive yet my Sunday journey back was via public transport, which included an hour and a half's wait at York train station for the only bus of the day which took me to the bottom of the college drive, via every village en-route. This was before the time of mobile phones, let alone iPads and Facebook. So I would treat myself to a latté, terribly grown up, and find somewhere to sit with my copy of Horse & Hound. Secretly I was really people watching, a pass time which I still enjoy. The extra special journeys were if I had been packed off with a little parcel of pheasant sandwiches!

Serves One

Ingredients

Roasted pheasant,
cold and sliced

2 Slices of white bread

Butter

Salt

Mango chutney

Place the pheasant slices on a buttered piece of bread, sprinkle on a little salt, spread about a teaspoon of mango chutney on top, then close with the second slice of buttered bread. Cut in half, and if you really want to push the boat out add ready salted crisps.

Voilà, you have one of the best sandwiches in history!

Mrs Town and Mrs Green

Butter Roasted Partridges
Served with Herby Couscous Salad

Serves Four

Ingredients

4 Partridges

100g Butter

1 Teaspoon
fennel seeds

2 – 4 Limes

Juice of 1 lime

200g Couscous

200mls Stock

2 Shallots

2 Garlic cloves

Extra-virgin olive oil

200g Small vine
tomatoes (e.g. Piccolo
cherry tomatoes)

125g Asparagus tips

1 Mozzarella ball

1 Tin of chickpeas

Small handful of each
fresh herb; mint, basil,
flat-leaf parsley

1 Tablespoon
tomato purée

1 Tablespoon
red wine vinegar

1 Teaspoon
paprika powder

Sea Salt

Freshly ground
black pepper

*P*artridges are lovely little birds. The native greys are beautiful, but issues with changes in habitat, predominantly due to the expansion of farming practices, led to a drastic decline in their numbers over the past 50 years or so. Thankfully their population is back on the rise, I would however recommend only eating grey partridge from an area where they are sustainable, through specific conservation and habitat management. We were admiring some black grouse on the way down from the moor, just where the heather starts to turn into grassland, when I was bemused by the covey of smaller birds adjacent. My companion, a very knowledgeable retired gamekeeper, enlightened me to the fact that these grey partridges actually thrive in highland hill farming areas as this is more comparable to their natural habitat, rather than the arable areas we associate the species with. French partridges, commonly known as red-legs, are more colourful and ornate in plumage. Seen more often, as they are bred for shooting purposes, they are frequent offenders at sitting on the side of the road until the last moment, then diving out in front of your wheels, brood of chicks in tow. Whichever variety of partridge you have, the delicate meat is very well suited to the light and stimulating flavours of this dish.

For the Couscous:

Place the couscous in a large bowl, heat the stock and pour over the grains, then cover immediately with cling film and leave for 20 minutes, this will partly steam it. If you do not have any partridge stock available, pheasant, or that frightful cheat of vegetable stock made with boiling water and a cube is perfectly fine. In a little extra-virgin olive oil gently sauté the sliced shallots and crushed and finely chopped garlic until they are soft and starting to colour, then add to the couscous. In a small bowl whisk together; 1 tablespoon of extra-virgin olive oil, 1 tablespoon of red wine vinegar, 1 tablespoon of tomato purée, and the teaspoon of paprika powder. Once combined add to the couscous, along with the juice of 1 fresh lime, and mix well. Wash and halve or quarter the tomatoes, depending on their size, finely slice all the herbs, drain and rinse the tin of chickpeas, and rip up the mozzarella ball into 1 – 2 cm pieces. Add these ingredients to the couscous bowl and re-cover, refrigerate for at least 1 hour before needed to allow the flavours to develop fully.

For the Partridges:

In a heavy bottomed frying pan heat half
the butter until foaming, add half the
fennel seeds and then add 2 partridges.
Coat all sides of the birds in butter
and then brown before transferring to
a roasting tin. Repeat with the other 2
partridges. Any remaining butter can be
poured over the partridges in the roasting
tin. Depending on the size of your birds
and limes, place half or a whole lime in
each bird's cavity (if using a whole fruit
make some deep incisions through rind to
release the juice during cooking). Cover the
birds with butter wrappers and roast in a
pre-heated oven to 200ºC for 25 minutes.
Remove the butter wrappers and finish
off in the top of the oven to crisp up the
outside of the meat for 5 more minutes.

To Serve:

In a hot dry frying pan, griddle pan, or on
the barbeque, quickly cook the asparagus
tips until just starting to colour. Do not
over-cook, one of the worst things I have
ever eaten is soggy asparagus, it goes
from a crisp delight to an insipid mush
in milliseconds. Taste the couscous and
season with sea salt and black pepper, add
more herbs if you feel it needs it. Allow
the partridges to rest on a board for 10
minutes, covering them with a piece of foil
to retain heat, then carve the birds into
thin slices of meat. Scrape the couscous
salad out onto a large serving platter,
scatter the asparagus tip over the top, and
finish off by adding the partridge.

This is great eaten with the meat still hot
or completely cold as part of a summer
party, picnic, or in bait boxes!

Venison & Tomato Soup

This is a gorgeous soup, which is incredibly easy to make and a great way to use left-over meat from slow cooking a neck or saddle, say for the Venison and Beansprout Spring Rolls, or pinch some out when preparing a Game Pie. Using venison stock ensures the soup has a really deep flavour. You can substitute it with vegetable stock, but that will result in something a little more feeble, unless you are using summer tomatoes which are ripe and bursting with flavour.

Serves Four

Ingredients

6 Large vine tomatoes
(approximately 800g)

Extra-virgin olive oil

4 Shallots

3 Garlic cloves

500ml Venison stock

Big handful of
Basil leaves

Tablespoon
light brown sugar

Sea salt

Black pepper

Approximately 100g
of cooked venison
meat, broken up into
small pieces

Warm a generous lug of extra-virgin olive oil in a large soup pan. Peel and roughly chop the shallots, sauté them in the warm oil for a few minutes until starting to soften but not browning. Add the 3 peeled, whole cloves of garlic to the pan and continue to sauté for a few more minutes. Wash the tomatoes, quarter them and remove any hard green flesh at the top, then cut each wedge in half again if needed before adding to the soup pan. Gently simmer the tomatoes for about 20 minutes until softening and releasing their juice, stirring frequently to prevent them catching. At this stage add a heaped tablespoon of light brown sugar, mix well and continue to heat until fully dissolved. Add the venison stock, half the torn basil leaves, a teaspoon of sea salt, and several generous twists of black pepper to the tomatoes, shallots and garlic to form the soup. After a few more minutes transfer the soup to a liquidiser and blend until smooth. Now return it to the pan, add the venison meat and the rest of the torn basil leaves, check and adjust the seasoning, then simmer for 20 minutes. Try to prevent the soup from boiling as this will damage the flavour.

Serve in warm bowls with crusty bread to dip in.

All in a Season

I'm always really rather tired at the end of another shooting season, and ready for a rest. I find my dogs start getting a bit headless because they think they know everything better than me. Anyone who disagrees with this probably also never loses one animal during lambing. I start to get a little sick of dressing game, and wearing waterproofs all the time.

Within days I am however a bit lost and depressed, February and March tend to have some hard days in them. This is because in one season I will have got; sunburn, windburn, snowed on, heat stroke, dehydrated, drenched, bruised by hail stones, blown off my feet, lost in fog, incredibly intoxicated, cried, and laughed till I hurt. Actually that can all happen in one day up on Raby's grouse moors. The fact is that doing this is what makes me tick, and the people I spend time with are some of the most fabulous people I know. They aren't rocket scientists or about to change the world, but genuinely good people.

The year has different seasons though and as such different priorities, before I know it the grass starts to grow and we are in the throes of lambing at home, which brings its own challenges. Young dogs are then ready to start doing some serious training, this year I have two Labradors to work with, and a young collie. The dogs have always been my number one priority, and I do have a better relationship with them than anyone else. When the phone rings and I get the new dates for grouse days in August it simply continues, the excitement on the glorious 12th nevertheless is pretty special every year.

Mr Green loading on the glorious 12th 1965

Venison Sausages with Mushroom Sauce on Toast

I spent one summer holiday from university up in Northumberland in the old keeper's cottage which my mother rented at the time as a bolt hole. When she was a child, this was where the young dogs were sent from the home kennels in North Yorkshire when they were ready to start working on grouse. Shooting was attracting interest from anti's that year so a team of countryside security guards were employed, and conveniently installed in the cottage next door to me. They taught me to make this dish, which we would often have before a day up on the moor. You can make the sauce the night before if you are short of time on a morning, the longer it is kept, the stronger the mushroom flavour will be.

Serves Two as a hearty breakfast or lunch

Ingredients

4 Venison sausages

Butter

20g Plain flour

250ml Milk

Sea salt

Black pepper

150g Closed cup mushrooms

4 Slices bread

For the Sausages:

Fry, grill or bake the sausages as you prefer. I tend to pop them in a roasting tin, add a tiny drizzle of rapeseed oil if I think they are particularly lean, and bake at 200ºC for 30 minutes or so. Doing it this way means I can get on with something else and they are less likely to burn if I get totally distracted.

For the Mushroom Sauce:

Slice the mushrooms, approximately 0.5cm in width. Heat a knob of butter in a frying pan over a moderate temperature until foaming, then add the sliced mushrooms with a couple of pinches of sea salt and fry quickly allowing them to turn just golden. Remove the mushrooms from the heat and set to one side.

Make a simple white sauce using the roux method, just like for the Lemon Roasted Pheasant with Tarragon Sauce (page 53). Gently melt 20g of butter in a saucepan. Once the butter has become liquid swirl it round the pan and then add the flour, stir the flour into the butter with a wooden spoon, beating it smooth until it has all cooked in and is starting to look like a smooth dough, this needs to take 3 minutes as a minimum to ensure it cooks. Add the milk, about 100ml at a time, stirring it into the roux, allowing it to become a smooth sauce that's just coming to the boil before the next addition. You may not need all the milk, or you may need a splash more, you are in charge, get it to the right consistency of sauce and then stop. Now add several generous twists of freshly ground black pepper and the cooked mushrooms. Allow the sauce to simmer for at least 10 minutes before you are ready to eat, to fully infuse with the mushroom flavour.

To Serve:

Toast the bread, place 2 sausages per person on toast with the mushroom sauce ladled on top. Along with a cup of tea or coffee this is guaranteed to set you up for the day.

Wild Boar Sausage Rolls

*A*lthough England was always home to me, we lived in a variety of countries when I was young due to my father's work. As he was Dutch we spent several years in The Netherlands, which sparks thoughts of canals and windmills in most people. In actual fact there is a large hilled area rich in vegetation called The Veluwe. This supports a significant population of game, including real wild boar, as in boars living in the wild. I remember seeing the little, striped piglets wandering about in the woods and always being a tiny bit scared that a protective mother might ambush us from anywhere. They are actually quite a common sight in Europe and it is on my bucket list to go wild boar hunting. These sausage rolls really set off the profound flavour and texture of the boar, but work equally well with venison.

*Serves Four as part of
a picnic or lunch*

Ingredients

One portion of Rough
Puff pastry (page 16)

4 – 6 Wild
boar sausages

Plain flour

Plum chutney

1 Egg, lightly beaten

Take your suitably prepared and rested rough puff pastry out of the fridge and roll out to just a few mm thin. Cut into two rectangles approximately 30cm x 15cm. Carefully remove the outer skins from the sausages and knead the meat with your fingertips out into a long shape. Depending on the size of the sausages you will need two or three per rectangle of pastry. Roll the meat in plain flour, shaking off any excess before laying horizontally along the bottom half of the pastry, joining each sausage together. Spread several teaspoons of plum chutney on the lower half of the meat, all the way along. Now brush both the upper and lower edges of pastry with beaten egg and fold over the meat, sealing the edge by pushing down with your little finger. Cut each roll into 6 pieces, approximately 5cm in length and trim away any excess pastry. Place the sausage rolls on a lightly oiled baking tray, brush them with the remaining beaten egg, score the tops, and bake in a pre-heated oven at 200°C for 20 - 30 minutes until golden brown.

Game Broth

T his is a true family recipe which has had each generation's contribution added as it has been handed down. My mother suggested leeks instead of onions, as they give a better flavour. I have added in the soy sauce to improve the seasoning. It is called Game Broth as there are no hard and fast rules as to which meat you should use. Observe the same guide as with Game Pie however, if you are using more than one source of meat; for each dark meat add a light meat. Venison and duck won't really work, but duck and partridge will, remember it's all about balance.

Serves Eight

Ingredients

1000mls Stock made from any game, preferably the same as the meat that you are adding to the broth (see page 18)

200g mixed lentils, including barley, split peas etc.

2 Potatoes

1 Swede

3 Carrots

1 Leek

3 Celery sticks

Sea Salt

Black pepper

1 Tablespoon Soy Sauce

Small bunch flat leaf parsley

Cooked Game meat of your choice

Soak dried lentils overnight (or as per packet instructions) in cold water, and rinse before use.

Reserve the cooked meat from the carcass which has been boiled down for stock, there will be some which is easy to remove before the stock is made, and some more which can be harvested when everything is soft. Be very careful however with bird carcases as it is easy to get the small splintered bones in with your meat at this stage.

In a large soup pan gradually bring the stock to the boil and add in the prepared lentils. Grate the peeled potatoes, swede, and carrots and add these to the pan. The natural starch in the potatoes which is released during cooking will help to thicken the soup. Finely slice the celery and leeks and add these to the soup pan as well, then season with a teaspoon of salt and a few twists of black pepper. Reduce the heat, cover the pan with a lid, and simmer steadily for 1 hour.

Add more stock or hot water if the broth looks very thick. Now add the reserved meat, broken up into small pieces, and a tablespoon of soy sauce with half the flat leaf parsley, finely chopped. Stir well, and continue to simmer for 30 minutes. Taste the broth and adjust the seasoning with salt, pepper or soy sauce as necessary.

Serve in warm bowls with a little parsley on top, with crusty bread and butter as a hearty, warming lunch or supper.

Game Pasties

This is a great way to use up left over ingredients from dinner. The secret is to combine flavours that work well together, but that will often be what you will have had in a meal anyway, say pheasant, beetroot, and red onions. Don't use anything too wet and juicy such as fresh tomatoes as these will give the pastry a soggy bottom! Also you need something to bind it all together, for example creamy mashed potatoes, or my favourite: venison sausages, Yorkshire leeks (page 80), and butter beans. The pasties freeze really well so are a good stock pile when an emergency lunch is needed.

Makes 6 – 8
medium pasties

Ingredients

One quantity of rough
puff pastry (see page 16)

Cooked meat

Cooked vegetables

Cooked potatoes or
tin of beans

Double cream or melted
butter

1 Egg, lightly beaten

Place equal quantities of cooked meat and vegetables in a bowl together and add the potatoes or drain and rinse a tin of butter beans or cannellini beans instead. Make sure everything is sliced quite small so that you don't end up with just a chunk of one thing in a pasty, and combine well so that the ingredients are evenly distributed. Add a splash of double cream or melted butter if the mixture seems a bit dry. Taste and season the pasty filling if needed, you could even add some cheese at this stage. Now take the prepared rough puff pastry out of the fridge and roll out onto a floured surface until just a few mm thin. Using a 20cm plate as a guide cut circles out of the pastry. Spoon the mixed filling onto half of each pastry circle, leaving a 2cm edge around the outside. Brush the whole outer edge of the circle with lightly beaten egg and then fold the unfilled half over the mixture to create a classic pasty shape, seal the edges together by pushing them with your finger. Place on a lightly oiled baking tray, do try to keep the pastry intact so the filling doesn't leak out during cooking, and brush the outside of each pasty with lightly beaten egg. Bake in a pre-heated oven at 200ºC for 30 minutes until the pastry is golden brown.

Enjoy hot or cold, or freeze for later use. Of course you can make smaller pasties, different shapes, and be as adventurous as you like with the fillings!

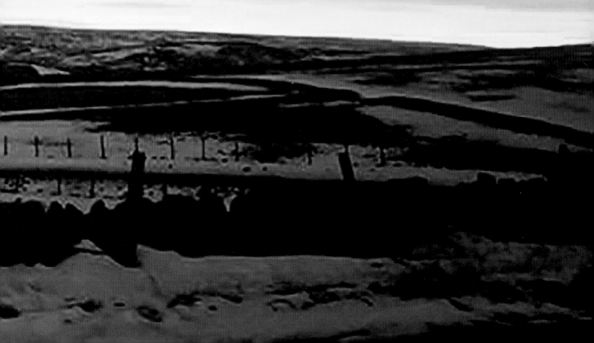

Something Sweet

Plum Jellies with Dark Chocolate & Cinder Toffee Biscuits

J elly is one of those wonderful things from childhood that everyone likes, it's great to devise an excuse of having small children to make it for so you can indulge. This version is for grown-ups and makes a lovely light dessert. The dark chocolate and cinder toffee biscuits are a bit sexy, and work really well with the jellies. We are lucky to have a selection of plum trees dotted around the farm so when in season I can just pick what I want, but if you have to buy them make sure it's a dark purple variety such as Opal to give the correct colour and flavour.

Serves Four

Ingredients

200g Red plums

300mls water

Juice of 1 lemon

2 tablespoons granulated sugar

1 sachet powdered gelatine

125g Dark chocolate (minimum 70% cocoa)

80g Unsalted butter

80g Cinder toffee

175g dark brown muscovado sugar

100g Plain flour

1 Egg

For the Jellies:

Rinse, quarter, and de-stone the plums, place them in a saucepan, add the water and simmer gently for 30 minutes until soft.

Puree in a blender and pass through a fine sieve, discarding the pulp. Return the juice to the pan, add the sugar and juice of 1 lemon and warm gently until the sugar has fully dissolved and been incorporated into the plum juice. Now dissolve the gelatine in 100mls of boiling water, whisk briskly until fully dissolved then add to the plum liquid.

Ensure the liquids are well mixed before pouring into four individual ramekins or jelly moulds. Cover each one with cling film and refrigerate for a minimum of 4 hours.

For the Biscuits:

Cinder toffee, otherwise known as honeycomb or the inside of a Crunchi, is just gorgeous. Usually bought in a bag of larger pieces it needs breaking up before adding to this recipe. To do this place the cinder toffee in a strong plastic bag and give it a couple of whacks with a rolling pin. If you are too overzealous you will end up with dust so go steady. What you want to achieve is small nuggets of sticky gold appearing through the chocolate.

Place the dark chocolate and butter together in a mixing bowl and warm over a pan of simmering water until melted together. Alternatively, for those daring enough, place the bowl in the microwave, heating for 30 seconds then stirring, before heating again, and so on until the chocolate and butter have melted. The key is not to heat for too long or too hard to prevent the chocolate from burning. Add the sugar to the bowl and stir until fully dissolved and a lovely chocolatey syrup forms.

Remove the bowl from its heat source and fold in the plain flour, then the lightly beaten egg, before finally combining in the broken up cinder toffee. Chill the biscuit dough in the fridge for 1 hour.

The biscuit dough will be pretty hard by now so use a sharp spoon to remove 50pence piece sized balls of dough. Evenly space them out on two baking trays lined with greaseproof paper, allowing enough gap for expansion as the biscuits cook so that they don't stick together. Bake in an oven pre-heated to 180°C for 15 minutes and allow to cool completely before removing from the paper.

To Serve:

Turn the plum jellies out onto individual plates with the chocolate and cinder toffee biscuits on the side, and eat with a small spoon. To make them look a bit special you can spray the tops of the jellies with edible golden shimmer spray.

Dressing Up

Life in the country is wonderful, we produce our own food, breathe fresh air every day, and don't have to deal with the throng of public transport and the commuter rat race. When your young dog picks its first bird, or you are watching the sun rise over purple heather on an August morning, there is a feeling that I can only describe as 'being so alive'.

Be under no illusion mind, it can be incredibly hard! Despite gale force winds, snow, hale, torrential rain, or baking heat the work still needs doing. There are dogs to exercise, shoot days to work, sheep to feed, and when you just want to sit down and cry because another pet lamb has snuffed it, you've got muck up to your ears, and the rain has got through to your pants, you just can't because dinner needs cooking! That's why a lot of my suppers are easy to make and can be prepared in batches so you have something in reserve for a bad day.

Every so often throughout the year though we get a chance to dress up, to shake off the staple wellies and waterproofs, tame the quad bike hair, tone down the wind burnt cheeks and head to an auction mart dinner dance or hunt ball in a pretty dress and high heels. I am not too ashamed to admit I did once fall asleep after the races in a bar, fascinator and heels still intact. More often than not however us country girls scrub up pretty well and dance 'til dawn.

So when you are getting a little down trodden and tired, do a bit of dressing up! The same goes for supper, why not add a bit of the sumptuous, sweet, glittery, and downright debaucherously good at the end of the day.

Heather Honey & Cardamom Ice Cream
Served with Hazelnut and Almond Biscotti

T he clean clear taste of heather honey, combined with warm earthy cardamom is a match made in heaven. Cardamom is traditionally used for its qualities in aiding digestion and to freshen breath. Scoop the ice cream up with the crunchy biscotti, and you have the perfect end to a meal.

Serves Four

Ingredients

5 Egg yolks

100g Caster sugar

3 Tablespoons heather or 'moorland' honey

1 Teaspoon cardamom seeds, pounded

500mls Crème fraîche or 250mls full fat milk and 250mls double cream

125g Plain flour

115g Caster sugar

1 Teaspoon baking powder

50g Whole hazelnuts

50g Whole blanched almonds

2 Eggs

Do not despair if you do not own an ice cream maker, I have given you an option for parfait or traditional ice cream here. Parfait contains un-cooked eggs, so is not suitable for pregnant ladies, and will melt quicker than traditional ice cream, it is however absolutely gorgeous and very easy to make. Traditional ice cream takes slightly longer to prepare and is a little more tricky, plus the correct apparatus is necessary. The biscotti also allow for some variation, try all one nut or a combination of the two as I have done here.

For the Parfait:

Beat the egg yolks, sugar, and honey together in a large bowl until pale and thick. Fold in the cardamom and crème fraîche, just enough to combine the ingredients without losing the air out of the mixture. Then transfer into a suitable container and freeze for at least 12 hours, or until needed.

For the Ice Cream:

Mix 250mls of full fat milk with 250mls of double cream and the cardamom seeds in a saucepan and scald, this involves heating the mixture until just boiling (i.e. the bubbles are just starting along the edges) and then remove immediately from the heat. Allow the mixture to cool and become fully infused with the cardamom for 30 minutes. In a separate saucepan beat the egg yolks with the sugar until combined and then pour over the milk mixture, whilst stirring. Continue to stir whilst gradually heating the mixture for about 10 minutes, to form a custard which is thick enough to coat the back of a wooden spoon, but do not allow it to boil or you will create scrambled eggs! Now allow the ice cream mixture to cool completely before adding the honey, mix this in thoroughly and churn and freeze in an ice cream maker, according to the apparatus' manufacturer's instructions. Transfer to a suitable container and pop it in the freezer until needed.

For the Biscotti:

In a large bowl mix the plain flour, sugar, and baking powder. Add the nuts and toss well to ensure that they are coated in the flour, this will stop them sticking together or sinking during cooking. In a separate bowl lightly beat the eggs, then add them to the flour, nuts etc., and fold in until evenly combined. Divide the dough between two baking trays lined with greaseproof paper to form equal oblongs approximately 10cm wide. Place in the oven, pre-heated to 180°C and bake for 30 minutes. Remove the biscotti from the oven and turn the temperature down to 140°C. Once the soft biscotti loaves are completely cool place them on a board, and with a very sharp knife cut into 0.3 – 0.5cm slices. Place these back on the lined baking trays and return to the cooler oven for 20 minutes. The biscotti will crunch up further once they have been removed from the oven and allowed to cool completely.

To Serve:

Serve the ice cream in bowls, with the biscotti alongside.

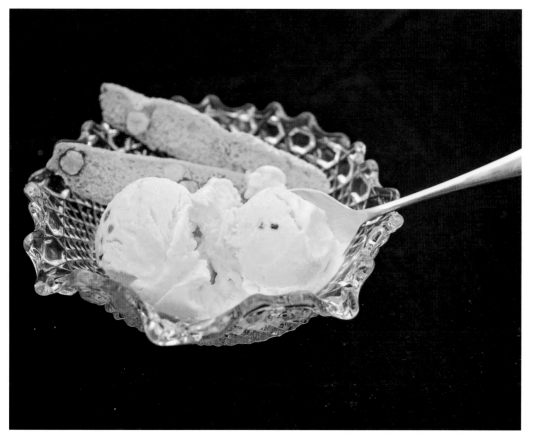

Sloe Chocolate Sauce

S *loe Chocolate Sauce stands on its own here as you can add it to any of the other desserts in this little section of the book. In fact, it is great with just vanilla ice cream. The sloes give a sharp tang to the chocolate, and the whole experience brings a naughty smile to your face.*

Serves Four

Ingredients

120g Sloe berries
(fresh or frozen)

50mls Water

100g Dark chocolate
(about 60% cocoa)

10g Unsalted butter

1 Heaped tablespoon
golden syrup

In the late autumn when the sloes are ripe I pick as many as I can, they've even come home in a woolly hat on the front of the quad bike before! What I don't use straight away or put in gin, gets frozen in portions. Then when required just submerge the little package of berries in hot water and they are ready to use.

Rinse the sloes, place them in a small saucepan with the water and bring to a simmer over a moderate heat until the berries burst and turn into a soft mush. Rub through a sieve back into the pan, discarding the pulp. Return the pan to a gentle heat and add the broken up chocolate, butter, and golden syrup. Allow all the ingredients to melt slowly together, stirring often and making sure the sauce gets warm enough to combine it without letting it boil which will damage the flavour.

To Serve:

Serve warm, and yes you may be excused for licking the spoon!

Essie's Mess

When I was little I used to pour maple syrup over vanilla ice cream and sprinkle chopped walnuts on top for a pudding, which was surprisingly good. The dish has developed a little since then, but I still get called Essie at home and as a distant relation to Eton Mess it remains a very easy dish to construct.

Serves Four

Ingredients

Vanilla Ice Cream

2 – 4 Ripe Pears

100g Walnuts

90g Granulated sugar

30g Unsalted butter

1 ½ Teaspoons cornflour

2 Egg whites

120g Caster sugar

For the Meringues:

Separate the eggs and place the whites in a clean, large mixing bowl. The yolks can be used to make ice cream or if I have a dog who has been working particularly hard they get added to their dinner as an additional source of protein. With an electric whisk beat the egg whites until they form a white semi-solid foam, reminiscent of cotton wool. Now add half the caster sugar to the bowl and beat until shiny peaks form in the mixture. Add in the other half of the caster sugar and beat again until those shiny white peaks re-appear and stay formed when you tip the bowl. When this has been achieved place dessert spoon sized dollops on two baking trays lined with greaseproof paper. The meringues don't need to be particularly neat as they are going to get broken up in the final dish anyway, but do try to make them a similar size to ensure even baking. Place in an oven, pre-heated to 110ºC and bake for 2 hours. Remove the meringues from the oven and leave them on the baking trays to cool completely before use. The meringues will keep very well in an air tight tin for a couple of weeks.

For the Butterscotch Sauce:

Place the 90g of granulated sugar in a heavy saucepan and heat slowly, without stirring, until all the sugar has dissolved and it starts to turn into a golden caramel. It may take a while to begin with, but then there is a fine line before the sugar burns and your sauce will taste bitter. So have patience and keep a close eye on the pan. Add 90mls of boiling water (from the kettle) to the pan of sugar and heat for a few minutes whilst stirring vigorously until the sugar has dissolved into the water. In a separate dish blend the cornflour in 30mls of water and then add to the caramel, allowing it to boil gently. Finally add in the butter, cut up into small pieces and stir until completely combined, and a thick and shiny sauce forms.

To Serve:

Peel and core the pears, then slice
lengthways and lay in the bottom of each
bowl, depending on their size allow half
to a whole pear per person. Add a scoop of
vanilla ice cream (good quality bought ice
cream is fine) and a broken up meringue
to the bowls. Then pour over the warm
butterscotch sauce and finally sprinkle with
chopped up walnuts. For extra indulgence
some whipped cream can be added on top.
It really doesn't matter what these look like
as they taste fab!

Sloe Gin

Finally, the essential potion in any country cook's kitchen or cellar! It is really not that difficult to make Sloe Gin, but it does benefit from a little TLC in the early days, and time. These days people like to add all sorts of flavours in, I'm always intrigued to know what's in someone's hip flask. Personally I like mine very simple and mature, the brown syrupy stuff is the best! Traditionally sloes should not be picked until after the first frost, and I have also been led to believe that each berry should be individually pricked prior to use to enable the flavour to release. Recent mild winters have meant that the sloes have been devoured by birds or are well past their best by the time we've had a frost. The point of waiting until after the frost is that this bursts the skin of the berries, so pricking them is a laborious and pointless task. The way round all this confusion is to pick the berries when they are lovely and plump and ripe, usually around the first week in November, wash them and freeze them for a few days before use.

Ingredients

300g Sloes frozen
(naturally or in a
freezer) and defrosted

200g Granulated sugar

600mls Gin

Place the sloe berries in a sterilised large jar with a rubber sealing ring, such as a clip-top Kilner jar. Add the sugar followed by the gin, and tightly close the jar. Store the jar in a dark place, and shake carefully every day for the first week or two until all the sugar has dissolved. Decant into bottles after 3 - 4 months by straining through a funnel lined with muslin and allow the sloe gin to mature for at least another 6 months. I keep the gin-soaked sloe berries in the jar for future use in cooking.

After the required time has passed, add to the shoot lunch basket or fill your hip flask and drink responsibly!

Acknowledgements

There are lots of people who have helped me along the way in making this book become a reality, some won't even know that they have. Special thanks are in order for the following people:

David Lee, the most fantastic taste tester and my most severe critic, thank you for always believing in me.

Mr and Mrs Charles Williams, and Mrs Trudgeon from Caerhays, and William Town and Fiona Kirk for allowing me to print my memories.

Lindsay Waddell; chairman of the National Gamekeepers Organisation, thank you for your support, photographs, and pushing me that little bit further.

Richard Dodd; gamekeeper, for the contribution of photographs, and all the other gamekeepers for just being who you are.

To Tania Still, my good friend and talented artist for painting 'The Captain' for the front cover of this book.

Dawn Caroline Smith, for the amazing food photography, a steep learning curve but great fun.

Tad (Evelyn Armstrong) for Bambi on the Pull.

All the staff on Carl's Fruit and Veg stall on Northallerton market on Wednesdays and Thirsk market Saturdays and Mondays, for your enthusiasm, encouragement, and finding me exactly what I want.

The staff at Yorkshire Game, for providing the game that I don't dress myself.

The team at Orphans Press for your dedication and expertise in design and printing to create this beauty.

For Mrs Green; my grandmother, teacher, and friend.

Index